HOW TO START A *SUCCESSFUL* HOME BASED WORD PROCESSING BUSINESS

Marianne T. Bradley

91-7212

International Information Associates/Yardley

Library of Congress Catalog Number 90- 083339
Bradley , Marianne T.
How to Start a Successful Home Based Word Processing Business

ISBN 0-945510-05-5

International Information Associates
P.O. Box 773, Morrisville, PA 19067 U.S.A.

Current Printing (last digit):
10 9 8 7 6 5 4 3 2 1

Printed in the United States of America

ABOUT THE AUTHOR

Marianne T. Bradley is the founder of a successful word processing service. The business, now almost six years old, was started from scratch, and today is quite profitable. She is an honors graduate of Bucks County Community College in Newtown, PA.

Because of her entrepreneurial efforts, she was listed in *Who's Who Among Students in American Junior Colleges.* She has received recognition awards from The Control Data Institute, the Lanier Corporation, and the Pennsbury School District in Bucks County.

Table of Contents

CHAPTER 1

WHAT BUSINESS ARE YOU IN?

That may seem like a pretty dumb question to ask, particularly since you bought this book to help you get into a home based typing service business. It really isn't such a dumb question though. You'd be absolutely amazed at the number of highly paid executives, working for major American companies who cannot answer that question. Sure, they know that their company makes computers or garbage cans, or whatever, but that may be only the product or service they sell, *not* the business they're in.

Well, if all these high priced executives of profitable companies can't answer the question, why should you worry about it? After all you just want to be able to do some typing for a few people and earn a few dollars right? Right!

Still you're just getting started, and most new businesses fail. These new businesses fail for several reasons, and high on the list of why they fail are these three:

- *not knowing enough about the business they just entered, and*
- *not having a plan which helps insure success in that business.*
- *not having enough money to grow the business*

Now, before we get into the details of what you need to run your home based typing service in a way that will make you money, let's look at the business, and the plan. If you have never been in business for yourself, *do not skip this chapter.*

1

Actually, if you have tried before and failed, go through this chapter anyway. See if the reason why you failed isn't in here.

WHY START YOUR OWN BUSINESS?

You are going into this business to make money, and to be on your own. Because you will be on your own, in some ways the information in these early chapters is probably more important than the detailed information on word processing business in the rest of the book.

WHAT AM I SELLING?

So your in the typing business?[1] No problems here. All you need is a typewriter, or a word processor, or a computer, some paper and that's it. Well, yes and no. The product you supply may be thought of as the finished typed page. Whether that page was done on a typewriter, or on a computer should matter very little to your customer, but as you'll find out, that's only partly true. To be precise, it may be true for some customers, but it may matter a great deal to others. In fact, even the paper you use will be important to some customers. Why? The answer is that you are not *merely in the business of supplying a typed page. You are also providing a service to your customer which goes well beyond that page.*

---

1 These comments are written specifically referring to a word processing business. They could refer to *any* business from a lemonade stand to a biotechnology laboratory.

WHAT BUSINESS ARE YOU IN?

CHAPTER ONE

You say, "I don't want to be in that service, all I want to do is provide typed pages. What's wrong with that?" Nothing really. In fact, many people do just that. If all you want to do is keep busy, and make the kind of money you would make with any part time job, then by all means provide only typed pages. *Face one hard fact: WHAT YOU GET FOR NOTHING, IS NOTHING.*

Please don't be mislead. It is highly unlikely that you will ever get rich from a home based typing business regardless of what services you supply. You can, however, make more money than enough to cover your costs and a little bit more. *You can make enough, with hard work, to provide a reasonable second income for yourself and your family, and you can do this with the convenience of being your own "boss."*

YOU'LL NEVER KNOW ENOUGH

One of the three major reasons why new businesses fail is, as I mentioned, not knowing enough about that business. Actually, this is not just a problem for new businesses but for those already established, including some of the giants in the *Fortune 500*. It happens to them when they put someone in charge of a division or company, who may have been the "superstar" of a different division, but who may not have a clue about the new business he or she has been asked to run.

It may happen to you because, although you may have been the best secretary there ever was, that's not enough! That you were the best secretary that ever was will certainly help, but if you've had no managerial experience you could still fail. I am not suggesting that you go out an earn an MBA before you start your home typing service.[2] What I am recommending is that you learn as much as you can about managing a business in general, and as much as you can about your particular business—word processing.

Purchasing and reading this book is a great start. Remember, however, no single book—no matter how good—can teach you everything. You should end up

---

2 MBA's without additional background and experience are often useless anyway.

3

after reading this or any other book with some new knowledge, and some questions you didn't have before you read the book.

So how do you get the knowledge you will need to survive in today's highly competitive business world?

There are several ways:
- *Read books on business*
- *Read magazines and other business periodicals*
- *Take courses at your local Community College*
- *Talk to other people working from home and others who are professional managers*
- *Join your local Chamber of Commerce and stay in touch with Home Business and Entrepreneurial Groups*

BUSINESS BOOKS

Book reading is perhaps the most economical way of learning new things. Relatively inexpensive, a book will always be there to refer to, day or night. There are books specific to your business, such as this one. In addition, there are texts on any topic relevant to running a business. These include:

Patti and Frazer's *Advertising: A Decision Making Approach* **The Dryden Press, 1988.**

Stanton and Futrell's *Fundamentals of Marketing* **McGraw Hill, 1987.**

Balsley and Birsner's *Selling: Marketing Personified* **The Dryden Press, 1987.**

Siropolis' *Small Business Management* **Houghton Mifflin, 1986.**

Lesikar's *Basic Business Communication* **Richard D. Irwin, Inc. 1982.**

Smith, Klein and Stephens' *Accounting Principals* **McGraw Hill, 1983.**

Mescan, Albert, Kendouri's *Management* **Harper & Row, 1985.**

These are just a few texts on the fundamental aspects of every business. I am not suggesting that you run out and buy a copy of each of these books. I am also not suggesting that you read them from cover to cover. What you should do is spend some time at your local library, and refer to the books in that way.[3] When you do find one that is particularly useful to you—consider buying it. For example, *Basic Business Communication* m e n t i o n e d above is pariculary good to have around in a home based word processing business. It is full of examples and suggestions on just about any business document you may run across, from letters to reports. The book also covers puctuation, grammar and layout of pages. It's a great reference you should have at your finger tips.

As you browse through the business section of your library, keep notes of other titles which may contain specific information which could help you understand specific business practices you may come across as your business grows. For example, Lanier's *The Rising Sun on Main Street: Working with the Japanese* (International Information Associates, 1990) will help you deal with Japanese c u s t o m e r s, should you be in a part of the country where Japanese investment has caused an influx of J a p a n e s e people. Sharp's *C o r p o r a t e Downsizing,* (International Information Associates, 1989) will help you understand how people who have been layed off—your resume customers—really feel.

Also keep in mind, that information about how to run a succesful business may be cleverly hidden throughout the rest of the library!

3 Naturally, your library may not have these exact titles—
    they will however have others on the same topics.

4 typos in the
first 5 pages of
this book !

This hidden information can be found in the biography and history sections. Think about it. One of the best ways to be successful is to imitate the actions of others who have been successful. It doesn't matter whether these successful men and women were political leaders, generals, or scientists. The reason why Thomas Jefferson, Marie Curie, Benjamin Franklin, Mother Theresa, Albert Einstein—even Caesar Augustus— were successful at what they did was because of their dedication and the methods by which they did what they did. To understand how you can be successful also, read their biographies and apply their methods to what you are doing.

While you can find many of the books mentioned at the library,[4] there are some books which you *must* have at home for reference. These include:

- *A good unabridged dictionary of the American language.*
  - *A good thesaurus*
  - *A grammar handbook*

Don't cheat yourself on the purchase of these three basic reference books. Buy good ones, they last virtually forever. There are three other reference books you should get. These are available in paperback, and are relatively inexpensive.

---

4 By the way, if the local branch of your public library is limited, ask them to get the book for you from another library, or visit the library at your local Community College. If you have trouble finding a book at your local bookstore, ask them to "special order" it. If they refuse, find another bookstore, good one's will.

Strunk and White's *Elements of Style* Originally published in 1935, the paperback is published by Macmillan, and its 85 pages will help any writer—including you and your customers.

Karen Elizabeth Gordon's *The Well-Tempered Sentence*, published by Ticknor & Fields in 1983 and subtitled *A Punctuation Handbook for the Innocent, the Eager, and the Doomed*, this little (93 page) book is a fun way to check correct punctuation.

The third book is also by Karen Elizabeth Gordon. This book is called *The Transitive Vampire: A Handbook of Grammar for the Innocent, the Eager, and the Doomed.* Published by Times Books in 1984, its full of fun examples of English grammar. Gordon's books are probably the only one's on grammar and punctuation you can actually read, and probably enjoy!

As your business grows, you may find it necessary to have specialized dictionarys, such as Stedman's *Medical Dictionary, The Penguin Dictionary of Science,* or others, depending on the nature of your clientel. Remember these reference books are important. *You will be expected, by many of your customers, to know correct punctuation, to use correct grammar, and to know how to spell, and to use correct form.*

One final thought on reference books. Some computer based word processing programs come complete with a built-in dictionary and a grammar checker. In order to use these effectively, you must know when to *avoid* the suggestion made by the computer. Unless you are capable of having memorized all the rules of our complicated language, you will still need the reference books. Do not depend solely on computer grammar and spell checkers!

BUSINESS MAGAZINES

Magazines and other periodicals, such as newspapers, are also a good source of up-to-date business information. Once again, you don't have to subscribe to every business publication there is. *Use your library.* If you do find one you particularly enjoy, subscribe to that.

Chances are, you will not find any specific references to home based typing services in the nation's business press. What you will find in magazines such as *Fortune, Business Week, The Wall Street Journal,* and *Entrepreneur* are articles by and about successful businesses and business people. Look for things you can adapt to make your own business successful. There will be a lot.

While we're on the topic of magazines there is one type you should read regularly. A computer magazine. Sooner or later your business will be dependent on computers in order to remain successful. While using a computer is easy, if you know the rules, there will be times when something will happen that will require more knowledge than simply turning the machine on and pressing some keys. Computer magazines are a great source of tips from other users and from computer experts. In addition, they are full of ads for programs and hardware add-ons. By reading these ads[5] you'll know what programs do what, and what you should pay when you buy one. Find one you like and subscribe, try *PC Magazine, Byte, Personal Computing,* and decide for yourself.[6]

There are many other specialized magazines which can help you. In fact, there is a magazine on almost any topic that you can think of, even on topics you would never

have thought of. When you're in the library, browse through *The Reader's Guide to Periodical Literature*, you'll see what I mean.

There is, for example, one magazine that you might want to consider reading regularly. It's called *Publish!*. In later chapters in this book, you will see that several of the most profitable products your home based word processing service can offer, if you have a

---

5 Also read the software reviews.
6 If you are a computer novice, don't be discouraged if you don't understand much of what is written at first. After a while you'll be amazed at how much you'll pick up simply by reading.

computer and the right programs, are "typeset documents. These include such things as letters, resumes, flyers, and brochures.

The problem with providing these services is that computers and desk top publishing programs make page layout and design relatively easy—usually just a matter of pushing a few keys or dragging a mouse. So easy that the design of the page is often very bad. *Publish!* shows how to do things properly, so that your results, with some hardwork and study, will be truly professional.

GO BACK TO SCHOOL—ARE YOU KIDDING?

One very effective way of learning more about what you need to know to survive in business is to go back to school. No kidding! Most areas in our country are within driving distance of a community college. These two year institutions offer everything from single courses in how to operate a

PC in their continuing education programs to Associate's Degrees in almost any major study area you can imagine.

Perhaps you already have a degree in sociology, or history or physics, you would need to go back to school like a hole in the head. Wrong, just like your study in your major area, you need specific information about how to run a business. People will not beat a path to your door because you have a "better mouse trap," not in today's business environment! First of all, they have to know your mouse trap is better (marketing), then they have to know how and where to get it (advertising). You have to know what your competitors are doing and offering (more marketing), and you *must* know if you are making a profit (accounting).

None of these things just mentioned are obvious knowledge to all people. Sure much of it[7] is common sense, and *seems obvious* after you've heard it. Remember most business courses (and the texts) are a compilation of the experience of the people who write the books, and give the

---

7 Except certain accounting practices

course.   Remember most new businesses, large and small, well-funded and backed by "cookie jar" money, fail for the same reasons. Lack of knowledge about their business, business practices in general, the lack of a plan, or not enough money. Go back to school, if you can afford it.[8] Take one course, specific to what you need to know, or study for an Associates Degree in Business Management,[9] it will be a good investment no matter what you do later.

JOIN A CLUB AND LISTEN

Talk to other people who are running their own small businesses. Listen to what they did right or wrong and use it. As you start your typing service, you will find that many of your customers are owners of small businesses. Usually they don't have enough

work, or simply can't afford a full-time secretary. These people will give you lots of practical information. Just talk to them, AND LISTEN. Chances are, some of your neighbors are managers in larger companies around your area, some may even be senior managers. Even if you don't know them very well, approaching them as "expert mangers" will flatter

them, and most will be happy to help out, once in a while.

---

8 By the way, most Community Colleges are a bargain.
9 At many of these schools you can major in small business management—try that at Harvard!

Finally, a good way to meet people with similar interests would be to join your local Chamber of Commerce, or other business or entrepreneur club. At their weekly—or monthly—meetings, you will meet many small business owners. It's a good way to become known to the community. At the same time you can pick up pointers from people who've travelled on the same road your travelling! You may also meet your competitors. Remember they are competitors, not necessarily enemies. Be nice. You'll, as well as they, will be able to check your prices and services.[10] You may also find that some will refer customers to you if you offer a service they do not. You should do the same also, if the opportunity arises. You will have a very happy customer for your services, if when they want something you can't do, you are able to refer them to another who can.[11]

10 Not fix prices, that's illegal
11 Just be sure that when you refer a customer to someone else, be sure you know the quality of their work. If you don't know the quality, say you don't know. You can say that you know they provide the service that the customer is looking for, but you've never seen their work. Remember their poor quality could loose a customer for *you*.

Chapter 2

═══════════════════════════════

What's Needed to Get Started and Keep Going

What Do You Have?

When you decided that you were going to begin your typing business perhaps you already owned some equipment. If so, more than likely you own either a typewriter or a home computer, or perhaps a dedicated word processor. If you do, your business will start with what you own. But before we get into the equipment, there is one thing you *must* have and that's a plan.

The Plan

In his book, *Think and Grow Rich,* Napoleon Hill[1] says:

> *that proceeding without a plan is like trying to steer a ship without a rudder, you may get where you're going without it, but chances are you'll end up wrecked.*

He's right. Now your plan doesn't have to be the size of your local phone book, neither does it have to be written in a style which can be read by others.[2] You should

---

1 Read the book, it's in paperback and it could change your life.
2 Unless you intend that it will be read by others.

write it down in some form however, so you can refer to it, and *change* it later.

MONEY

The first thing you should decide is how much money you have to invest in your business, this is your *starting capital. Remember one of the prime reasons why new*

home based word processing business, but as long as it's home based that prospect is unlikely. If the business grows to the point where you need and can afford an office in a small office park, or perhaps a store front in a mini mall, then the likelyhood of you making bags full of money increases. You can, however, make a good second income from your own home.

businesses fail is the lack of enough money to allow the business to grow. In the case of a home based typeing service, this is not an over-whelming problem. The capital needed to start such a business, and keep it going is relatively low. As in most businesses which require a low capital outlay, the return on this investment is also relatively low. Sure, you can become a millionaire by starting a

Your capital will be used in two ways.

   1. To buy necessary equipment, if you need it.

   2. To buy operating supplies.

Let us suppose you have $1000 (including credit on credit cards) you can use.[3] You could spend it all on equipment, but then where

---

3 Without taking food off the table.

would you get the money to buy paper, ribbons, envelopes, etc.? If you have some equipment, you may want to upgrade a few items. If you have less money, *regardless of what you may need spend less.*

Remember everything you spend on your business will determine whether you are making money. *So you must watch what you spend.* As you know from your home budget, money has a habit of flying away. You will probably need about $400 - $500 for supplies (this assumes you are starting with no supplies), which should carry you the first month or maybe longer. On the average, after your initial purchases, your outlay for supplies, should be under $200 per month. It will get higher as your business grows, but shouldn't be more than $200, if you buy wisely. After your income exceeds $1000 per month this outlay for supplies will grow also. Remember to buy only what you need, *when you need it.* Never overbuy, especially when your business is new.[4]

The rest of your money can be used to invest in equipment and programs for your computer. These are expensive and should be purchased with care. Details will follow in later sections.

SETTING A GOAL

Knowing how much money you have to invest, and therefore what equipment you have or will get, you can now write down your objective. This is a very simple statement of where you want your business to go. It should sound something like this:

" By such and such a date [insert a real date] one year from now, my word processing business [insert the business name if you have one] will be bringing in $1000 in sales per month [or whatever target you think is appropriate], in return for these sales, I [we] will offer error free service, at reasonable rates, at the fastest speeds possible."

The reasons for the statement being a definite as posiible is that this is the *goal* you will be working to achieve.

---

4 Always, however, have a few spare parts like a ribbon or cartridge for your printer, and a few extra diskettes if you use a computer.

Any decisions you will have to work will be made against this goal. If you have a choice of **A** or **B**, and **A** brings you closer to the goal, and **B** doesn't then you choose **A**. It can be that simple. As you business grows, and you learn more about it, you objective will broaden, and how you will meet that objective [the part starting "...in return for these sales"] will become more detailed and complex. But for now that simple statement will serve as a business plan.[5]

If you are a reader of self-help or time m a n a g e m e n t books, you know that one of the biggest obstacles most of us have to overcome is *procrastination*. In terms of running your own business, procrastination translates into the inability to make quick and decisive decisions. The inability to make clear decisions has been said to be a problem for many people. Why is this?

Think about your own life. There have been times when it was easy to decide a question, other times it has been agony. If you think real hard about the differences in the two situations, it is likely that the easy decision came because you knew *exactly* what you wanted. It was only difficult to decide when you couldn't be sure, for whatever reason, what you really wanted. The difference between procrastination and decision is often just the presence or absence of a goal.

There is one other complicating factor. If you read the goal just given for your word processing business, you will note that it is isolated—it refers only to your business life. You may have other important goals, both business and personal, which may be as, or more important. For example, you may want to put your son or daughter through MIT, or you may want your business to evolve from a typing service to a local community newspaper. Such goals must also be taken into ac-

5 For more on goal setting, and a positive attitude read the book by Napoleon Hill mentioned above.

count. Once you have more than one goal, you have a potential problem.

Prioritization

Now, what do you do with this apparent problem? If your life was simple and all you had to do was get $1000.00 per month from your typing service, then picking A over B is easy—but what about college tuition? Should you spend $3000 on a computer if you need the money for the mortgage? Depends.

The simple way to avoid conflicts because of multiple goals is to prioritize them. Simply decide which is the most important and it becomes #1, the next important becomes #2, and so on.

You can do this by asking yourself a few questions regarding each of your goals. The questions are:

What will happen to me if I don't achieve this particular goal?

Which of the goals will offer the highest payback.?

Who will bear the consequences if I don't achieve this particular goal?

Which of the goals that I have to deal with is most important to me, my family, etc.?

Although these questions are quite simple and are not, at first glance, complex, think about your answers carefully. Once you know which of your goals is most important to you—once you know what you really want—then making decisions is really easy. Once you have the goal, and can make decisions then failure will be impossible.

BUDGET

Next you need a budget table which keeps track of your income and expenses by month. It should look like the one shown on the next page. This document will be important to you, as it lets you know if your on track to your goal, and whether you are making any money. Simply, you are making money if income (sales) is greater than expenses. If it is the other way around you're losing.

At the risk of offending those people for whom creation of a budget table is trivial, let's explore the example table in some deail.

As you can see, the table is a summary of the money that comes in, and is spent by your company on a monthly basis. You could

ACME WORD PROCESSING SERVICE
A TYPICAL FINANCIAL SUMMARY 1990

INCOME

	JAN	FEB	MAR	APR	MAY	JUN	JUL	AUG	SEP	OCT	NOV	DEC	TOTAL
WORDPRO	622	425	952	1238	707	225	478	578	899	1254	1265	1008	9650
TYPESET	39	206	190	184	228	321	125	100	189	205	363	124	2274
SPRD SHEET	125	250	175	189	219	100	285	217	333	564	152	201	2810
MAILINGS	0	0	0	0	0	25	50	200	125	36	178	255	869
RECEIVABLES	-455	-323	-125	-255	-125	-225	-100	-125	-68	-89	-45	-78	-78
NET SALES	330	558	1192	1357	1029	446	838	970	1478	1970	1913	1510	15525

EXPENSES/PAYMENTS

	JAN	FEB	MAR	APR	MAY	JUN	JUL	AUG	SEP	OCT	NOV	DEC	TOTAL
BANK FEES	0	3	0	0	17	0	0	17	0	0	8	12	56
DUES/SUBSCR	0	10	14	115	5	0	0	0	21	0	0	23	188
POSTAGE	10	50	25	10	15	0	9	21	0	18	45	21	224
MARKETING	41	25	50	0	100	0	0	0	125	0	0	250	591
ADVERT	150	172	150	150	125	125	125	125	125	125	125	125	1622
SOFTWARE	0	169	0	35	55	0	0	0	0	88	0	0	347
FEES	10	0	0	0	10	0	0	0	0	0	0	0	20
PRINTING	0	125	0	0	0	0	0	0	0	0	224	0	349
SUPPLIES	130	108	281	247	185	85	156	289	157	289	121	45	2094
EQUIPMENT	0	0	0	0	270	0	0	0	0	0	0	0	270
REPAIRS	0	207	0	0	34	0	0	0	0	0	0	0	241
TELEPHONE	10	5	13	12	14	8	9	15	3	9	0	2	102
UTILITIES	25	20	20	20	20	20	20	20	20	20	20	20	238
AUTO	25	20	12	2	14	8	10	4	9	8	18	6	136

ADJUSTED PROFIT/LOSS

	JAN	FEB	MAR	APR	MAY	JUN	JUL	AUG	SEP	OCT	NOV	DEC	TOTAL
RECEIPTS	330	558	1192	1357	1029	446	838	970	1478	1970	1913	1510	13590
R'CEIVABLES	455	323	125	255	125	225	100	125	68	89	45	78	2013
TOT.SALES	785	881	1317	1612	1154	671	938	1095	1546	2059	1958	1588	15603
OP.EXPENSES	396	914	565	591	863	246	329	491	460	556	563	504	6477
OP.PROFIT (LOSS)	389	-33	752	1021	290	425	609	604	1086	1503	1395	1084	9125

1ST Q	2ND Q	3RD Q	4TH Q	1ST HALF	2ND HALF
1108	1736	2299	3982	2844	6282

keep this table on a weekly or a biweekly basis, but that would probably become to cumbersome as the business grows. You should however keep it on a monthly basis, any longer period of time and you will loose control of your business. If this table is kept using a spreadsheet program on your computer (see the section on Software), then the totals in the last column will be automatically updated as you add new figures at the end of each month.[6]

Before we look at the numbers and how they are calculated, let's refer to the words in the first column. You can see that the table is actually divided into three sections:

Income

Expenses/Payments

Adjusted Profit/Loss

The totals of each of these sections represent the parts of a simple formula you need to compute to know whether you are making money—a profit, or loosing money—a loss. The formula is :

INCOME - EXPENSES = PROFIT

Under INCOME there are six headings in this example. They are:

WORDPRO - represents sales for a particular month from your typing service.

TYPESET - represents sales for a particular month for work which was "typeset".

MAILINGS - represents sales for a particular month for preparing mail lists.

---

6 One benefit of keeping such a table is that it forces you to review your situation on a monthly basis. Remember the sooner you find a problem, the easier it is to fix.

RECEIVABLES - represents money owed to you by your customers. It is generally a negative number. It can be zero if everyone has paid their bill and nothing is owed you or even positive if cutomers have paid in advance.

NET SALES - represents the cash which you brought in during a particular month. It is simply the number (sum) you get by adding the other four numbers. Remember, adddding a negative number means to subtract the value.

This particular income example breaksdown sales by type. You don't necessarily have to do that. For example, line 1—WORDPRO— could be used to represent *all* sales for the month. However, if you do offer different categories of products, it is a good idea to break out their sales as shown in the example. This will help you determine which products are appealing to your customers, and which are contributing most to sales and profits. It will also let

you know, at a glance, whether an investment you made, say a desktop publishing program, is paying for itself in increased sales.

As an example, look under expenses for the month of May in the table. You will see that Acme Word Processing Service spent $125 for software. They invested in a mail list program in order to offer mail list services. Beginning in June, you can see modest sales for "Mailings" at $25. Sales continue in this category and by December a total of $869 was made in "Mailings." Buying the progam was a good investment.

Now let's look at the Expense section. As you can see, there are 14 different categories under Expenses. Each one of these represents a type of expense necessary for running your business. The last line in this section shows the total expenses for the month. As before, you could have only one line for expenses. If you did that however, would you really know how you spent your money? For example, look at February in the example. The total expense for that month was $914. That's quite a bit of money to have spent.

If all you used was a one line entry for expenses—914—you don't know very much. You would have to go through all the receipts you've kept for purchases[7] to find out exactly where the money went. If as you spend money, you add it to its proper expense category you will be able to tell where you've spent at a glance.

Although most of the categories in the expense section should be reasonably clear, let's review each one in case the shorthand of the spreadsheet is confusing.

BANK FEES - represent all payments you have made to your bank for checking account[8] fees, etc.

DUES/SUBSCRIP - represents all payments for dues in professional organizations, like the Chamber of Commerce, and the costs of magazine subscriptions, and books like this one.

POSTAGE - the cost of stamps, permits, P.O. Box, etc.

MARKETING - represents payments for your marketing efforts. This may include such

---

7 Always keep all receipts whenever you buy something. The IRS will love you for it.
8 Open a separate business account for your business. The IRS frowns on mixing personal and business money. If you operate your business under a fictitious name, like *Acme*, check with your state government for how to register the name. You'll need a certificate from them in order to open the account in the company name.

things as surveys, market profiles, or customer prospect lists.

ADVERTISING - the cost of placing your ad in the local newspaper, or Yellow Pages, etc.

SOFTWARE - the cost of buying any computer software necessary for your business to function or grow.

FEES - the cost of any fees you have to pay the government, or your tax accountant to get all this in shape for the IRS.

PRINTING - the cost of printing any sales brochures, business cards, letterhead, etc.

SUPPLIES - the cost of all your operating supplies, like ribbons, ink cartridges, light bulbs, etc.

Generally anything that is consumed in running your business.

EQUIPMENT - the cost of your computer, typewriter, copier, etc. Generally anything you buy for your business which is not consumed over a period of a few years.[9]

REPAIRS - the cost of repairing any items associated with your business.

TELEPHONE - the cost of all business calls.

UTILITIES - part of the heat, electicity, and gas cost of your household. It should be proportional to how much you

---

9 Because of your personal financial position and some IRS rules you may elect to *depreciate* the cost of some of your equipment over the life of the equipment rather than expense it all at one time. Ask you tax accountant. Given the nature of a home based word processing business, expense everything you can. The profits will be lower when you buy major equipment, but you did spend the money! Stay on this *cash basis* unless recommended otherwise by a professional accountant.

use for your business. Your tax accountant should be able to help you estimate the proper amount.

AUTO - a mileage charge for the business use of your personal auto. Your accountant will be able to tell you how much you can charge per mile.

The final section in the table is ADJUSTED PROFIT/LOSS. The first item in this section is Receipts. This is the same number as the Total Net Sales from the first section. Now in this section, unlike the first, we are concerned with the total sales for the month, not just the cash received. To get the Total Sales (line 3) you must add back the receivables which were subtracted in the Income section. If you now subtract the Total Operating Expenses from the Total Sales, you get the profit for the month. Notice, if the expenses are greater than sales, see February in the table, the result will be a negative number, in the example $33. *This is how much money Acme lost in February.*

The bottom two lines in the example table are just sums to give you a better snapshot of profit and

loss as you progress through the year. The "1ST Q" number is the profit for the first three months, in the example $1108. The "1ST HALF" is the profit for the first six months—$2844. The table shows that Acme made a profit of $9125 for the year on sales of $13590— not bad!

You probably have noted that all the numbers in the example are *whole numbers.* Naturally, all sales and all expenses didn't come in as nice round whole dollars. Unless for some reason you or your accountant wish this summary to be accurate to the penny, round off to the nearest dollar. It's a lot easier, especially if you're doing these calculations by hand.

Remember if all your customers pay right away, and you have a policy not to bill anyone later,[10] then the Receivables entries shown in the example are not necessary— and the calculations are then much more simple.

Expect to loose money for a while. *ALL BUSINESSES LOOSE AT THE START. The greater the investment*

---

[10]Which is probably best during the first year.

you make at the beginning, the longer it will take before you begin to show a profit.

INVOICES AND STATEMENTS

Every time you finish work for a customer, you should prepare an invoice—a bill showing the charges— for presentation to the customer with the finished work. You can mark the invoice "PAID", for the customer's records and yours, with a rubber stamp.

Remember to make at least two copies of each invoice, one for the customer and one for your records.[11] As with most other chores, there are computer programs which will automatically invoice on pre-printed forms. Most of these will also do all the bookkeeping, also. Until your business is established, there is no reason to purchase such a specialized program. You can effectively keep your books manually.

FIGURE 5.1

TYPICAL INVOICE

Acme Word Processing
123 Main Street
Anytown, USA
999-555-1212

INVOICE

Date:_____
Invoice Number:___

SOLD TO:_____

_____

_____

Item	Quantity	Description	Price	Extension

11 Some customers may require three copies for their records.

There are some very easy to use bookkeeping record books which you can buy for less than $20 at your local stationery store.

You could also buy pre-printed invoice forms. Using your word processor, you could prepare invoice blanks, and fill them in as necessary.

should describe how many of each item was sold, its base price, and the extension of the price for the number sold. Figure 5.2 shows a completed invoice.

For those of you who extend credit to your customers, that is,

FIGURE 5.2
COMPLETED INVOICE

Acme Word Processing 123 Main Street Anytown, USA 999-555-1212	**INVOICE** Date: February 23 1992 Invoice Number: 234

SOLD TO: Mr. Joe Smythe
456 17th Street
Anytown, USA

Item	Quantity	Description	Price	Extension
A	2	Business Letters	2.25	4.50
B	1	Double Spaced Page	1.75	1.75
		TOTAL		6.25

The Figure 5.1 shows the kind of invoice you can use and what should appear on it. Your address and phone number should appear at the top. You will find that the invoice is often used by previous customers to call you when they have new work. There should also be a date, and an invoice number. *Never use the same invoice number more than once.* The invoice

you bill your regular customers at the end of each week, or month, you will also need a Statement. The statement is merely a summary of all the purchases made by a customer during the previous billing period. Figure 5.3 shows a typical, completed statement.

Note that the statements boldly requests PAYMENT ON RECEIPT. For the most part, customers pay. Should you have a customer who

FIGURE 5.3
TYPICAL STATEMENT

Acme Word Processing
123 Main Street
Anytown, USA
999-555-1212

STATEMENT

Date: February 29, 1992

Payable on Receipt

SOLD TO: Mr. Joe Smythe
456 17th Street
Anytown, USA

Item	Invoice	Description	Date	Amount
A	234	Word Processing	2/23/92	6.25
B	242	Word Processing	2/25/92	8.75
		TOTAL		15.00

is slow in paying, you must be persistant—keep sending statements. The customer may be forgetful or having a bad day, so you really don't want to antagonize them. You also want to get paid. After the second week, or month has passed, and the customer still hasn't paid, type the following note on the statement.

FRIENDLY REMINDER!

If your remittance has already been sent disregard this notice. Thank you!

If it is necessary to send a third statement, the language of the message on the statement should become a bit stronger:

PAYMENT PAST DUE!

If your payment has been sent disregard this notice. Thank you!

Should it still be necessary to send a fourth statement, the message must be forceful. Something like:

DELINQUENT PAYMENT NOTICE

Repeated requests for settlement of your past due accounts have been ignored. Unless received within 10 days we will take immediate action to collect payment.

If you send a statement with a note like the last one, you must be prepared to do something, or backdown. At this point you probably have a Bad Debt. You can go to a collection agency, and pay them to collect— a good idea if the amount is substantial, or if you have a "Small Claims Court" in your area, you can bring suit for a modest fee. If you do this, make sure your records are in order. Just remember that winning such a suit doesn't mean you'll get the money. It still must be collected.

If your customer is merely a slow payer, and you know it, you wouldn't want to send the delinquent message. Merely send the second message over and over until the slowpoke pays.[12]

In all businesses, there are bad debts. You will get bad checks, and there will be people who don't pay. Try not to take it personally, it's just another expense. It has been said that you can expect up to 10% of sales in bad debts.

But take heart, it has been my experience that most people are honest, especially if you treat them honestly.

---

[12] Then insist on payment before you deliver the next batch of work.

CHAPTER 3

EQUIPMENT—THE RIGHT TOOLS FOR THE JOB

TYPEWRITERS

Let's begin with typewriters. *By the way, all this assumes that you can type. If you can't, you really shouldn't be in this business.* If the equipment you own is a typewriter, particularly an older electric typewriter, the business will be very difficult. If you own a manual portable typewriter it will be almost impossible to provide a perfect page *at a cost which will allow you to make money.* If this is the position you're in, you will have to consider buying different equipment. We'll talk about what kind in a later section.

What happens if you can't afford to buy new equipment right now? If you're an excellent typist, you will be able to produce excellent pages, regardless of what equipment you use. Whether you can produce them at a cost which will allow your business to make money is doubtful. No matter how fast you are, revisions on a typewriter still take time, and use supplies. It doesn't matter whether these revisions are necessary because of a mistake made during the typing, or whether the changes are necessary because your customer changed his or her mind.

Most typewriters are just not equipped to make major changes. Certainly, typewriters with self-correction tapes can make minor changes. Of course, there's always corrections fluids such as Liquid Paper©. *Never use correction fluid.* Okay, almost never. Correction fluids are acceptable for drafts, and informal typing. *Correction fluids should never be used on a final copy.* Remember your customer has brought the job to you, and is willing to pay you, primarily to get exceptional quality, error-free pages.

The real problem with trying to use a typewriter as the prime piece of equipment in a typing service business is the speed and the cost to *you* when making major revisions. If your customer wants to move a paragraph, or remove some information in the middle of a document, you will have to re-type the entire thing. That means the customer has to wait, *and every customer behind that first one has to wait also.* You can see that it wouldn't take many corrections of this sort to have dissatisfied customers, or have you working through the night to catch up.

There are other things you can't really do efficiently with a typewriter. For example, even for a well-trained experienced typist,

statistical typing—long, complex tables of numbers—is not easy. At the very best it is time consuming. Remember you are now in a business. The faster you get through a job, and the more times that job is right the first time, the more profitable your business will tend to be.

Other simple things like documents that are required to be "landscape" may be impossible if your typewriter's carriage is not wide enough. Footnotes, like the notes throughout this book, require careful planning with a typewriter, particularly if there is more than one on a particular page.

There may be other things which are impossible to do on a typewriter, even if you have one of the newer, full featured electronic models. Things like:

- *changing pitch*
- *changing* typeface
- *bold* **print**
- *multi-addressee letters*
- *right justified text*
- *special symbols, e.g.,* © ® £
- *foreign text, e.g.,* ç â ¿

If you could be sure that all your competitors, both the current ones and the new ones which will come along, would have a typewriter just like yours, then few of the things mentioned would really be a problem. Your potential customers would get the same level of service from everyone. Chances are, however, that someone in the area will have a word processor, or a home computer. That means they will be able to do things you can't. *Then, all other things being equal, they will get the business.*

If all you have is a typewriter, and you don't have the money to invest in different equipment right now, go ahead and start anyway.[1] Sure it will be difficult, things will take more time, and there are somethings that you just won't be able to do. Starting, will however, generate some money, and if you can save that money you can buy the new equipment. One final thought on your typewriter, resist the urge to throw it out, or trade it in— keep it. The typewriter has uses, even in the most sophisticated typing service businesses, as you will see later.

Now, let's talk about some of the equipment you will need to establish a successful word processing business. Business theory says: "The more you spend, the more you'll make." This is true—up to a point. If you spend *wisely*, only when you need to spend, and only when you can be reasonably sure that the business will pay for the expenditure in a reasonable amount of time, then that old adage is true.

As you read through the rest of this chapter, remember you don't need to buy any of the things mentioned right away. As your business grows, and demand for certain products or services occur, you can buy the things you need at that point. Keep in mind that one customer's request does not necessarily create a demand—unless that customer has assured you of business equal to or greater than the money you needed to spend.

WORD PROCESSORS AND COMPUTERS

Some of you may own dedicated word processors. These are as good as most "low end," or inex-

---

1 Remember *never* procrastinate, if you want your own business, just do it.

pensive computers, better than some in fact. These word processors make revisions easy. Like computers, actually they are computers, you can see your work on a screen and correct it before the document is actually printed. There are some limitations such as:

- *page size*
- *font capabilities*
- *landscape pages (on some)*

The biggest limitation of these machines is that the only thing they can do is word processing. As we will see later, this limitation can

restrict the potential income of your business. But if this kind of device is what you already own, be happy. You can operate a successful typing service business.

There is a good chance that the reason why you have decided to get into a home based typing ser-

vice is because you own a personal computer (PC). As you may know, there are computers and there are computers. You can, however, be successful in your business regardless of the make of computer you own.

If you already own a PC, you probably own one of the following:

- *Commodore, e.g., 64, 128, or Amiga*
- *IBM PC or a compatible from one of many manufacturers*
- *Apple or Apple MacIntosh*
- *Atari (the computer not the video game)*

If the computer you own does not fit into one of the above categories, I apologize for not mentioning it, but you may have a few problems in dealing with the rest of the world. If you own a PC you are in good shape to start your business. Depending on which type you own you may be in better shape for certain aspects of the business than others.

How about the problem of buying a computer? There are so many choices, and the machines are so technically complicated, it may seem like an impossible problem to solve. But let's try.

If you are *computer literate*, you probably have already made up your mind as to which computer is best. I will not try to change your mind! If you have no idea what to buy, I will give you my choice. Naturally, I have my prejudices also. With respect to Commodore, and Steve Jobs and his *Next*®computer[2], there are really only two practical choices: Apple and IBM (and its compatibles).

Once upon a time, not too long ago, Apple computers were probably a good choice. They were simple to use, and did all sorts of neat things. But Apple decided to be sure that no one else made an "Apple type" computer. So today, you buy an Apple from Apple or you don't buy it. This means that things are not as inexpensive as they might otherwise be.

IBM type computers, at the beginning, were more difficult to use. They were also incapable of doing some of the things that Apple computers could do—especially when it came to graphics. But that has changed, IBM or compatible computers, i.e., MS-

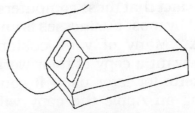

DOS systems, are now every bit as easy to use as Apples. They can also now handle all the graphics and page layout work that used to be only the province of Apple computers.

IBM "clones" are made by lots of companies, and because of this you can get real bargains. If you are going to buy a computer today, you should seriously consider an MS-DOS computer, that is, an IBM or a clone. The reasons why are:

2 The *Next* computer system is great. It's not compatible with anything else, however. If you and Steve Jobs were alone in the world, it would be an excellent choice.

- *they are simple to use*
- *they are relatively inexpensive*
- *they are fast*
- *they can do anything you will need to do*
- *they are used by most businesses in this country*

The fact that these computers are used by most businesses is important. Many of your customers may want a copy of their work on diskette for later use. If you are using an Apple the copy will be useless to them.[3] They may want to give you data, such as addresses, for example, and these are likely to be MS-DOS based.

Today, there are many "Shells" which make using MS-DOS computers as easy as an Apple. A shell is a program which pops up when you turn on your computer and allows you to do things without necessarily knowing what commands to type. Just like an Apple you can use a mouse and point at

a word or picture, click a button and whatever is supposed to happen, like copying a file or formatting a disk, happens! There are many such programs: two of the best are Microsoft Windows® and GEM Desktop®. We use GEM,— it's almost like using an Apple— and it's inexpensive, only around $40.00 or free if you buy one of their other programs. We also use Windows on one of our computers, simply because

we have some programs that won't work any other way. I should mention IBM's new operating program, meant to replace MS-DOS, at this point—it's called OS/2®.

This expensive new operating system[4] is graphics oriented, like GEM and Windows. It will allow you to do more than one thing at one time. It also has a few housekeeping tricks which MS-DOS left

---

3 Unless you have a relatively expensive piece of add-on harware which can convert one format to another.
4 An operating system is a program which allows the computer to do things like run programs, or send data to a printer.

out. This system will only run on a few PC's (expensive ones) and is meant to replace MS-DOS. There are millions of MS-DOS computers out there and more are sold each day. Except for very large companies, who seem to like wasting money, the only benefit of OS/2 is to IBM. It will help them make train loads of money if everyone follows along. If you need to run more than one program at one time, try Windows 3.0, it works well.

WHAT COMPUTER TO BUY

If you are buying a computer for the first time, and agree that you should buy an IBM or a clone,[5] then you should know that there are essentially 5 types of MS-DOS computers. These are:

- *the "8088"*
- *the "80286"*
- *the "80386 SX"*
- *the "80386"*
- *the "80486"*

These numbers are the designations of the computer chips, which are the heart, or the brain if you prefer, of the computer. As you go from the 8088 to the 80486 they become more powerful, and faster. They also become more expensive.

The 8088 (and the 8086) are the original models. They are somewhat slow and outdated. However, if you are severely limited in the amount of money you can spend, this is your choice, regardless of what a  computer salesmen may say. For the basic business, the limitations will be few, and if it's all the money you have, don't overspend. Our word processing business still has the original 8088 we purchased years ago—it still functions, and a lot of our word processing work still goes through that machine.

5   Unless you have lots of money to spend, don't buy an IBM. If you decide to buy an Apple or any other type I can't help you.

The ideal machine for this business is a 286. It's fast, powerful and you can probably get one for only a bit more than an 8088. If you can afford it, buy it. Its speed and memory capabilities are good.

The 386 is a powerful, fast machine. It is an excellent choice for a word processing business doing complicated page layout and graphics. It may be something you want to purchase later, after the business can justify the purchase.[6] The 386 SX is less expensive than the 386 and somewhat less powerful. If you budget won't allow a 386 but you need 386 power, consider a 386 SX. The 486 is new, extermely powerful, and very expensive. It is probably not a good investment for you business.

COMPUTER SPECIFICS

Regardless of what you own or buy, your machine should have a minimum of 640 K internal memory, one 3-1/2" floppy drive, one 5-1/4" floppy drive, a 20 Mb hard disk (minimum), and a high quality monitor (color or monochrome, depends on your preference and pocketbook). This will give you maximum flexibility.

6 Of course by then 486's may be cheap, and the "786" may be the top end machine!

The 8088 should cost you (with the add-ons) between $600-1200. The 286 should cost between $1000 and 2000, the 386 between $2000 and $5000.[7]

PRINTERS

Assuming you already own a PC, the most important piece of hardware that you need for your home typing business is a printer. All other things being equal, it is the capability of the printer that determines the quality of the output. Remember your customer only sees the output from the printer, they don't know how fast your computer is!

There are four basic types of printer:

- *Daisy Wheel*
- *Dot Matrix*
- *Ink Jet*
- *Laser Jet*

DAISY WHEEL PRINTERS

Daisy wheel printers are called that because the print is provided on some sort of disc or ball type element which resembles a flower. These printers give excellent quality alphanumeric[8] characters. They are exactly the same as any good typewriter. The wheels are changable so that many different typefaces are pos-

7 Prices change quickly, check them thoroughly. Your local computer stores will generally cost more. Try Radio Shack, especially when they have a sale. You might also consider mail order. The prices are excellent, and the products quite good, Appendix 1 lists some mail order computer suppliers. All our computers were purchased in that way. Look through the computer magazines, you'll get a good idea of who has the best prices. Go through the back issues to see whose been around for a while, and find the dealer who will service the computer should something go wrong, preferably at your location.
8 Numbers and letters.

sible. If this is the printer that you own you can provide excellent, high quality pages.

There are several drawbacks to daisy wheel printers, not the least of which is that they are slow. In addition they tend to be noisy, a minor problem associated with all impact printers[9]. They are also incapable of producing graphics. This may not seem like a big deal. After all you are in a *word* processing business. Remember there are additional services which your competitors may be able to provide, and that your customers may expect that include adding graphics to documents. These products, as you will see later, tend to be very profitable also!

Special symbols may be impossible, as well as, some important things you will occasionally encounter such as superscripts, and subscripts. Landscape text will be limited to the working width of the printer carriage. You can however,

make an excellent start in your business if this is what you have, as long as the work you get is strictly text.

DOT MATRIX

There are two types of dot matrix printers: 9- pin and 24- pin. What you need to know is that the more "pins" the better quality and the more the printer costs. Dot matrix printers are extremely versatile. If you own one of these, then you should be able to start your business with little trouble, *if your printer is capable of "near letter quality" NLQ print.* If you have one of the older versions of these printers that can do no more than perhaps double strike when not in the draft mode you will need to buy a new printer.

NLQ approximates the sort of type you would get from a typewriter, 24- pin models do a better job than 9-pin. Dot matrix printers, both the older and the

---

9 Any printer which strikes the page.

newer models, use the matrix pattern for letters for which the printer was named. These rectangular letters and numbers are the type we have all become used to on various digital displays on clocks, and calulators. The letters generally do not have true descenders and ascenders.[10] This means that formal types are impossible, and the quality of the documents you produce will probably not be good enough to compete. Appendix 2 shows some of the different types of print possible with a dot matrix printer.

LASER & INK JET PRINTERS

Ink jet and laser jet printers are the top of the line. They are also the most expensive and the most versatile. If you own any one of these you have nothing to worry about in starting your home based typing service, unless, of course you don't have the proper software to take advantage of your equip-

ment. See Appendix 2 for a type sample from an ink jet and a laser printer.

For MS-DOS computers, perhaps the most widely used printers are manufactured by:

- *Hewlett Packard (HP)*
- *IBM*
- *Tandy*

There are, of course, many other manufacturers of laser printers, and most of these emulate[11] HP or IBM. This ability to emulate, is very important. If you buy a laser printer manufactured by Panasonic, or some other company, it would be wise to be sure that the printer emulates one of the major brands. The reason for this is that many software programs are designed to run specifically with one of these printers, especially the HP Laserjet® series. Some "no name" laser printers, while excellent machines, may have difficulty using all the features of your

---

10 An ascender is the part of a letter which rises above the base height, such as on this "d". A descender is the part which drops below the base height, such as in this "g".

11 Run as though they were an HP or IBM printer.

program. If your printer can emulate one of the majors, it is a much simpler way to work.

There is a second type of laser printer which can be important to your word processing business. These are called Post Script®

should look. For complicated graphics, special effects like circular text, and availability of different typefaces, Post Script may be the best, but somewhat expensive, way to go. Examples of some of these things are shown in Appendix 2. Of course, considering

printers. Post Script printers are made by a variety of manufacturers such as:

- *QMS*
- *Texas Instrument*
- *IBM*

Post Script is the name of a computer programming language.[12] Specifically, Post Script is a page description language. It tells the computer inside the laser printer how the page it is about to print

their capabilities, Post Script printers may be considered relatively inexpensive by some. This is only true when they are compared with electonic typesetters which may have price tags in excess of $80,000. They are however, more expensive than normal laser printers.

Post Script printers range in price from a low of about $1200 to a high around $25000. The differences

---

12 A language is a set of instructions using its own grammar and syntax, which tells a computer what to do.

in this range are due to differences in such thing as resolution, memory, speed, paper handling, and whether the printer can produce color documents. For most of the work that you are likely to encounter in a home based word processing business, a Post Script Printer will not be necessary. However, if you find that your business is heavily into page layout and graphics, it may eventually be a good investment.

One thing to keep in mind when purchasing a Post Script printer is the printers ability to emulate others. Many Post Script printers cannot emulate any other kind of printer. This means it will not function with many computer programs that do not specifically support Post Script printers. Some can emulate a variety of other printers like LaserJet, Epson, or Diablo. Because your business will be doing many things, it is a good idea to have a Post Script printer which is versatile in this way. One excellent, high quality, high speed Post Script printer which emulates other types of printers is QMS' PS - 810 Turbo™. It sells for around

$5500, but is worth it, *if your business is at the point where it can handle such an expenditure.*

There have been several recent advances which will allow HP LaserJet, or compatibles, to emulate a Post Script printer. These are things like programs which translate your program's output into a format such that the HP will print Post Script effects. There are also some manufacturers of cartridges which plug into the HP and do the same thing. These range in price from $100 to $1000 (for the usual reasons). They are a great way to upgrade to Post Script capabilities when you need them, without loosing the investment in your original laser printer.

Ink jet printers such as HP's DeskJet Plus® may be thought of as a poor man's laser printer. For around $600 they will produce a similar 300 dpi output to a LaserJet. One disadvantage to this type of printer is that when the page first emerges from the printer, the ink is wet and easily smears. The ink is also not waterproof and will run if the page gets wet.[13] The printer is also somewhat slower than most laser printers, and its

13Recently, it has been announced that HP is working on a better ink—one that drys quicker and is waterproof.

limited memory prevents printing complicated pages. It is however, quiet, compact, and you can purchase a number of snap in cartridges which give you additional typefaces and memory. Best of all, it is relatively inexpensive and may be the best purchase for a small typing service.

WHICH PRINTER TO BUY

So what printer should you buy? If you are considering a dot matrix printer as your only printer, because of limited funds, then you should buy a 24 pin model. Remember most people don't like the look of dot matrix print on resumes and business letters, or any other formal document. I would also suggest that you shop around before you buy this printer (or any other one for that matter). Inexpensive printers often do not work with all software programs, i.e., they're incompatible. Stick with brand names like Epson, Okidata, unless you're sure your bargain can *emulate*[14] one of the better known brands.

If you can't afford a laser printer, which you really should consider[15], then you should take a close look at the Hewlett-Packard Deskjet Plus.® This ink jet printer gives excellent quality print. It sells for around $600. Later, you can add more memory[16] by purchasing a $200 cartridge. Different fonts can also be added later at about $100 per cartridge. It is probably one of the[15]for a home based typing service. It's quiet and versatile, take a close look at this printer. Appendix 2 shows a type sample.

SOFTWARE

WORD PROCESSOR

Let's talk about software[17]. There are a few things to keep in mind. The *one* type of software you need for your home based typing service is a word processor. Like everything else, there are word processors and there are word processors. Which word processors are the "best?" Depends on what you need, and what you get used to, for example, my original computer was the

---

14 This means act as if it was an Epson, etc.
15 Try the Tandy LP 1000 from Radio Shack
16 So you can print complicated pages with graphics.
17 These are the programs needed to run the computer

Commodore 64®. I thought Fleet System® was the best for that particular computer, at that time. Today, we use only MS-DOS® based computers in our business, and I think Ashton-Tate's Multimate Version 4.0™ is a great word processor. Most reviews of this particular program that have been written by the "experts" generally give this product bad marks. They think programs like Wordperfect 5.1® are better. We have it, and it does have some neat features that Multimate doesn't, but I'm so used to the latter, I haven't really used "5.1" at all. The point is, if you have a word processor you're used to, and it has the features you need, don't change. Just remember, this type of program is the cornerstone of your business, don't skimp on its purchase. Things will be a lot easier and more *profitable* with a full-featured program.

Here are some things that a full-featured word processor do:

1. It should be easy to use;

This means that the word processing program should be easy to use for *you*. If you have been working with Wordstar®, or Samna® for years, you are probably so used to that programs methods for doing things, that learning to use a new "easy to use" program may not be worth the effort. Switch only if the word processor that you are using cannot do some of the other things mentioned or if *you* truly think it is hard and akward to use.

2. It should allow variation in text style, and size within the same document.

In conjunction with whatever printer you may have, the word processing program should also allow you to vary the typeface, pitch, size, etc., of the print. Ideally, it should allow you to do these things within the same document.

3. It should allow you to draw boxes, and lines.

Because some people will want portions of their text set off by lines or boxes, your word processing program should permit you to draw these things on the page when you need them. The value of this should be obvious. The quality will be much better than if the lines are hand drawn on the page.

4. It should allow you to import pictures from other programs, ideally it should contain some of this artwork itself.

Some of your customers may want to add pictures to their text documents. These pictures are referred to as line-art or clip art. Your word processing program should have the ability too add such line art within the text. At the very least, the word processor should come with a selection of clip art pictures to use. Often, these word processing programs use their own proprietary format for generating these pictures. This may mean that you cannot use clip art from other programs, in other formats. If you think that you will be adding lots of pictures to your typing then be sure that your word processing program will allow you to import clip art in other formats from other programs. The kinds of formats most often encountered can be identified by their file extensions, i.e., the three letter code after the period in the file name—FILENAME.XXX. The most common one's are .PCX, .GEM, .HPL, .CGM .

5. It should be able to create tables of contents, and automatically create section numbers.

If you work for lawyers, and students, it is a blessing if your word processing program can automatically create section numbers, and tables of contents. This feature may be considered by some to be a luxury. Once you do several long documents which require sections to be numbered or lettered, or require a table of contents, you'll find that a program which can create these things will save you time and trouble—particularly after major revisions have been made in a document.

6. It should allow you to import data from other programs, such as databases and spreadsheets.

Your word processing program should allow you to import data created in other programs. For example, a customer may give you an address list created in a database program like DBase IV® or PC-File 5.0®, or the customer may give you a complicated table of numbers created by spreadsheet programs like Lotus 1-2-3® or Quattro Pro®. You'll save yourself a lot of time and loss of profit if these data can be brought directly into your word processor without re-typing. In addition, you may find it easier to prepare large data tables by using a spreadsheet program and importing the data than by formatting the table in your word processor.

7. It should allow you to import documents from other word processing programs.

Because you could not possibly afford to have each and every word processing program that exists[18] and customers may come to you with documents already prepared (on a diskette), whatever word processing program you do use should be capable of reading the formats of other popular programs. At the very minimum, your word processor should be able to read standard ASCII files.[19] You can then ask your customers to bring their data in ASCII format.

8. It should have a spell checker and a thesaurus.

Your word processing program can help minimize the number of times it will be necessary to revise a document if it has a spell checker.[20] Using the checker, typo's are more easily found and corrected. Many of the latest versions of the major word processing programs also have an electronic thesaurus.

This is useful for quick checks and revisions of words that may have been overused. Remember, neither will really replace the un-abridged books. [See the section on Reference Books]

*9. It should let you see exactly what you will print on the screen before you print it. This is the notorious WYSIWYG: "What you see is what you get." Usually what you get is WYSIAWYG: "What you see is **almost** what you get."*

Seeing what will actually be printed, before you print is important—to your profits. If you can see obvious errors before they are printed, you will save the time and the cost of printing documents more than once.

THE DATABASE AND THE SPREADSHEET

There are two other types of programs which would be a big help to you as you start your busi-

---

18 Nor would you want to even if you could afford it.
19 This is an agreed standard which should be common and easily transferable.
20 These can be purchased as separate programs also.

ness. They are not absolutely essential but they will help. These are:

- *a Database, and*
- *a Spreadsheet.*

What's a database? Think of a database as a giant file cabinet inside your computer. You can put anything you want in it.[21] You can file your customer's names and addresses, or mail lists for others. You can track your suppliers, your inventory. Almost any information you could list on paper you can put in a database. After the information is in, you can sort it anyway you'd like with the touch of a key. You can view it on the screen or print the list on

your printer, and if you want, you can print only part of it, any part you want. For example, if you have the information entered, you could print your entire customer list, or just those who have given you business in the last 30 days, or just those that live in a certain part of town, or all those whose last names begin with "W".

Now there are databases and there are databases. In the world of MS-DOS, DBase III+® is considered, by some, to be the greatest. Like all programs it has some problems with compatibility (it won't work with other programs), but it is powerful. It is also relatively difficult to use. There are some simple ones around (cheap, too!) like PC-

21 Just like a real file cabinet, if you file without following the rules, things quickly get out of hand, and you won't be able to find anything!

File 5.0®.[22] It can't do everything that DBase can, but it can do somethings that DBase can't. For a small business such as yours, it's probably more than enough.[25] It's easy to use without too many instructions. There are many inexpensive databases. Look around. Generally all you will need is one that will keep track of addresses and generate mail labels.

A spreadsheet is a kind of database for numbers. Spreadsheets can take these numbers and do all sorts of mathematical computations on them. There is the most famous spreadsheet of all Lotus 1-2-3®. It's powerful and expensive, and difficult to use. I would suggest that you take a careful look a Borland's Quattro Pro.® This is a spreadsheet that can do anything 1-2-3 can do. It does it just as well, uses less memory, and provides high quality printed tables and graphs.

Best of all, it is much simpler to use than 1-2-3 and is generally less expensive.

You can use your spreadsheet program for many things. It can be used for anything where you might be manipulating lots of numbers, and performing mathematical computations on those numbers. For example, you can keep your company budget on it, as was shown in Chapter 2. You could keep your household budget in the same way—or keep track of the value of your stocks and bonds.

Besides budget tables, there is one thing that a spreadsheet can do and it is directly related to the profitability of your company. If you find that you are doing a lot of statistical typing, especially with numbers, entering the data in a spreadsheet rather than using a word processor will make the accuracy of the document better, and proofreading much easier.

22 PC File 5.0 uses and generates DBase files directly. It is available as *shareware*, i.e., you can get it on line, from a service, or buy the disks for a few dollars apiece. If you need the manual you can then get it from the people who made the program— Buttonware in Bellvue, WA at 800-J-BUTTON.

Because the spreadsheet automatically does calculations,[23] after you have finished entering long columns of numbers, the spreadsheet will "tell" you if they have been entered correctly. This is true because the automatically generated sum should equal the sum that is on the sheet you are typing from. If the two numbers are not the same, there are only two possibilities—either you typed in the wrong number somewhere, or the customer made a mistake.

OTHER PROGRAMS

There are some other programs you might want to consider. When you have the money, they'll make life easier, and they will generate higher profits than simple typed pages.

PAINT & DRAW PROGRAMS

These are programs which allow you to modify artwork and create new graphics—freehand, or by modifying other line art. They are programs like PC Paintbrush®, and GEM Draw Plus®. They range in price anywhere from $50 to over $400 for very sophisticated programs like CorelDraw!®. When you decide to buy one, read the box. Be sure the program you buy supports your computer. Be sure your computer has enough memory, be sure your monitor is supported, and be *absolutely sure* the program supports your printer or one of its emulations,[24] otherwise you will never see any of the work you created.

FORM CREATION PROGRAMS

These programs, like Form-Tool™, make it easier to paint and print forms, such as invoices, order forms, etc. Some also allow you to fill out pre-printed forms using your computer. If your business is such that you are creating lots of complicated forms on your wordprocessor for your customers, then consider one of these programs. They will save you time. Lowering the costs for creating forms will have a positive effect on your profits.

---

23 When you enter the formula for the calculation in the right place.
24 These are things to check before you purchase *any* program.

ACCOUNTING PROGRAMS

This type of program will keep the financial records for your company. They will do journals, ledgers, expenses, invoices and statements, write checks, keep track of purchases, etc. Certainly, you can do all these things with a combination of your word processor and spreadsheet. You can also keep your "books" manually. During the first year or so, you can use your word processor to bill your customers. The rest of your records can be kept in a small business accounting book designed to make entries easy. You can find one at almost any stationery store for under $15. However, when your business gets to the point where your sales are over $1000 per month, you may have 300 or more customers, and a lot of transactions to keep. At this point, an accounting program will help. These programs can be expensive—especially the one's you buy in modules. Check the price of Bedford's Integrated Ac-counting™. It should be among the less inexpensive accounting programs. More importantly it's automatic, and easy to use.

GRAPHICS PROGRAMS

These relatively expensive programs will be useful to you, if your business does a lot of charts and overheads, and graphs. There are two excellent programs Lotus Freelance® and Harvard Graphics®. They will pay for themselves quickly if you have that kind of business. They save time and give excellent quality documents. I prefer Harvard Graphics, simply because it takes up less space on my hard disk than Freelance. It doesn't do quite as much as Freelance, however with the recently introduced Harvard Draw Partner® add-on it comes close, in fact, it does some things Freelance can't. Draw Partner is inexpensive and if your just buying Harvard Graphics you will now find that Version 2.3 has all the features, including Draw Partner, in the same package.

DESKTOP PUBLISHING PROGRAMS

These page-layout programs will be important to your business if it develops to the point where you are preparing newsletters, brochures, bulletins, and other such documents. Least expensive of these are programs such as NewsMaster® and PFS: First Publisher® either should be more than sufficient for most work you will encounter. There are, of course, more sophisticated page layout programs, notably Aldus PageMaker® and Xerox's Ventura Publisher.® Both cost in excess of $600 and will probably be more than you need. If you do need this level of sophistication, remember both are excellent. Except for personal preference, perhaps the only way to decide between the two is that PageMaker seems more suitable to short documents, while Ventura works well with longer documents.

CHAPTER 4

OPERATING SUPPLIES

YOU MEAN I HAVE TO BUY MORE !

I am sure after going through the last chapter that you are tired of adding up the money to spend in order to start your business. But as the saying goes "you get nothing for nothing." In fact, as was mentioned several times, for the first year or two, you may be spending quite a bit more on equipment, programs, and supplies than you are making. This is one of the prime reasons why a start-from-scratch enterprise takes so long to make a profit. If you have virtually nothing when you start, then any money you make has to be invested in the business. This will help the business grow by getting new, and hopefully more porfitable jobs. Starting a new business is not for the timid.

The things we will talk about now are your operating supplies. These supplies are generally consumable items which you need to operate your business successfully, on a continuing basis. They are things like paper, pencils, typewriter ribbons and other items. Don't be discouraged at this point all this money will come back to you. Generally if you are good at what you do and work hard at it, all your investment including that which you made in your computer and other (capital) equipment will come back to you probably after the first 10-24 months. What that does mean of course, is that for the first year or two you will be working merely to get back the money you invested into your business in the first place. You generally won't start to show a real profit until at least 18 months have gone by perhaps more. However, if you already own the equipment and the program, the time to profitability is shorter. Starting your word processing business will "pay" for the computer you bought last year.

One of the keys to making this profit is buying your consumables or operating supplies at a cost which allow you to make money. For example you can buy computer paper for your dot matrix printer from a computer supply store or a department store for about $8-10 for a package of 50 sheets. You can also go to a stationery department store, or to a mail order supply house and buy a whole case of the same computer paper, that is 5,000 sheets for around $20-35. You can see then the cost of the product that you are selling your customer, the cost of a single typed written letter can come down dramatically if you buy the consumable items correctly.

We are now going to go through a list of the major items that you will need for your home typing service in order to operate effectively.

PAPER

Remembering that you are now in the business of offering an excellent product which will bring customers back to you. The paper that you put their work on is therefore very important. You should not use photocopy paper for the originals that you give your customers. You must also realize that paper is not just paper. There are different types of paper for different types of machines. Good qulaity bond paper used for typewriters may not work well on a laser printer or on a laser jet printer. The paper companies have gone through a great deal of time and effort to develop papers which are designed for the new electronic printers. In order for your product to look its best you should take advantage of the money they spent. If you are using a dot matrix printer the paper you will use will be exactly the same as those used for a typewriter. You should use as a minimum a 20 pound bond paper. This means that when you buy paper for your dot matrix printer (the kind with the holes that run up the side: called pin feed paper) you should be sure that the paper you are buying is a 20 pound bond. Much of the computer paper sold in that manner is actually a much lower grade sometimes around a 16 pound paper and not bond. If you are using a dot matrix printer you should also buy and have available one ream of 24 pound bond paper (without the pinfeed strips) for special use. If you have a laser or laser jet printer you can also purchase 20 pound bond or heavier paper as long as you are sure that the paper has been formulated specifically for electronic printers. These electronic papers are also available in cases at extremely modest cost, most times no greater than any other quality paper. The color and brightness of these electronic papers are set to bring out the best that your printer can do. If you have both types of paper available you can run the same document off using the different papers the results will be obvious and striking.

In addition to this usual white paper you should also have available a higher weight paper—at least a 24 pound bond in white, ivory, and grey. This is the paper you will use for the preparation of resumes. Resumes are an extremely important product for your word processing business. People that come to you to type their resumes are coming primarily because they want their resumes to look good a fact which makes getting a new job easier. If you use a high grade paper for these resumes, and if you can offer the customer a choice of colors for the resume you will be offering an advantage over your competitors, telling your customer that you know your business. Because this sort of paper is expensive we would recommend that you buy and have on hand only one ream of each color. It is not necessary to buy this paper by the case unless it turns out that your business becomes a thriving resume preparation center. If that happens you should certainly buy this better paper by the case.

One of the things you should remember about paper, is that it can be ruined if it is stored improperly. Your paper should be kept in a relatively dry spot (with low relative humidity) and stored flat so that it won't curl. Not only will it make the printing and final product look more presentable, but it also will make life easier for you because flat dry paper tends to feed better through computer printers. Remember that you must also have matching envelopes with each type of paper that you offer to your customers. Never mix the quality or the color between the printed page and the envelope that you intend to send the page. Our experience has shown that you will generally need a lot less envelopes then you do paper. Most

51

people, except for those who come to you for resume preparation, tend to use their own envelopes.

TYPEWRITER RIBBONS AND INK CARTRIDGES

You will also need a supply of typewriter or printer ribbons and ink cartridges for your printer. As with the paper, these supplies should be the best quality you can reasonably afford. The reason for this with most other expensive options we recommend is that it directly affects the appearance of the product that you are selling. The better your product the more likely you are to attract and retain customers.

One thing to remember and think about these supplies is that you should always have a spare ribbon, ink cartridge, or toner cartridge in your office. These are the type of things that seem to have the ability to run "dry" at the most annoying times. It is much safer to have a spare on hand in case your local stationery store is closed when you desperately need one. You will also find that some of these items particularly ribbons are cheaper if you buy 6 at a time.

If you own a laser printer chances are there are other consumable parts to that printer which must be periodically replaced. In addition to the toner cartridge, the " ink " used by the laser printer there are generally other parts which are consumed as the printer is used. These other parts may be cleaner screens and the actual printer drum itself. While these replacement kits are relatively expensive, we would recommend that you keep a spare around for that emergency that always occurs with an important customer and at the time the stores are closed and you can't get replacement parts.

MISCELLANEOUS SUPPLIES

There are several other things which you will need around your office to keep you business functioning smoothly. These are things that will be used up and will have to be replaced periodically. They are generally not expensive, they don't seem important, unless of course you haven't got one of them around. Things which fall into this category are pens, pencils, paper clips, and rubber bands. In addition you should have a pair of scissors, a ruler, a three hole punch, some large manila envelopes and some manila file folders. You will also need a supply of blank 5-1/4 and 3-1/2 inch diskettes. These will be used for storage of your customers files even if you do have a hard disk.

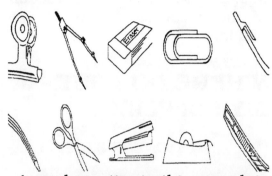

A good practice in this regard, is to download from your hard disk all your customer files to a floppy disk at the end of the each month. In this way you will be able to offer to your customer a free service of retaining their document for, a year, for any revisions that your customer may want to make, without tying up valuable space on your hard disk. After about a year it will also make it more simple to find these documents if they are filed on these disks by month. If all the work you have done is on the same hard disk for a full year it may be difficult to find that one letter Mr. Smith had you do for him eight or nine months ago.

There are other items that you may find convenient to have around as your business grows and you fall into a working pattern. These things such as: 3M's Post-it™ notes, a few extra stamps, rubber stamps for things that you have to keep writing over and over again. These are not absolutely essential at the start up of your business. As time goes on you will find lots of little things that will make life easier for you.

REFERENCE BOOKS

There is one final category of item you will find indispensable. These are your reference books. Although mentioned before, they are brought up again for emphasis. First among the list of these very important books is a dictionary. Get a good hard cover dictionary and be sure that it is unabridged. Do not try to use a paperback. In addition to a dictionary, you will find it important to have a Thesaurus. A book on English Grammar and a book on writing styles is also important and will help answer some very tough questions and allow you to help your customers out of some problems.

The best book on writing style which you can buy and is available in paperback and is only about 85 pages long. This book was written by William Strunk and E.B. White and is called *The Elements Of Style*.

As you business begins to grow and you get a handle for the type of customers you are getting you may want to think about obtaining several specialty dictionaries. These may be things like *Stedmans Medical Dictionary*, a dictionary on computer terms, or perhaps one on scientific terms or perhaps something like the *Merk Index* if you find that your business includes typing some of the long chemical names in use today.

HOW MUCH MONEY DO I HAVE TO SPEND FOR ALL THIS STUFF?

Basically expect to spend about $400-500 to stock your business for the first time. After that it should cost you only about $200 per month to keep your stock replenished. Remember however that the monthly expenditure will depend on how much business you get. The more business you get the more you will have to spend for supplies because they will be consumed. If you buy wisely, look for a bargain you will be making money. But the amount of supplies should be only a fraction of the dollar sales you will be making.

WHERE DO I BUY MY SUPPLIES?

STATIONERY STORES

One of the first places that you may want to check is your local stationery store. In this case we are not talking about a greeting card store but a real live genuine stationery store. Go in and talk to the owner of the stationery store tell him what you are doing and you maybe pleasantly surprised to find that he will be willing to offer a discount over the list price of the materials found in his catalogue. At the very least he or she will be an expert on all sorts of things which will be a big help to you.

There has been a recent change in the stationery business. If you happen to be lucky enough to live near one of the new stationery supermarkets, such as Staples, Inc. you will find that you can get many of these supplies inexpensively at one of these large stores. If you are shopping in these stationery supermarkets please remember that as with all supermarkets, be selective in what you buy. The things that are on sale or at a special price are there to bring you into the store. By all means buy them if they are the things you need. As you are wandering up and down the isles of one of these gigantic stationery stores be careful that you *don't buy everything* you are looking for from the store. You maybe able to get some things at a better price from another supplier. Remember what you spend on your consumable items will determine how much profit you make in your business. The trick is to buy as inexpensively as possible.

MAIL ORDER SUPPLIES

There are lots of mail order stationery supply companies in the United States, who will be happy to send you their catalog and the prices are generally good. As long as you remember to shop around so that you know a good price when you see one, and as long as you remember to check mail order houses catalogue to make sure that what you are buying is what you want then this is a good way to save money on supplies.

Also remember that materials ordered this way may take a few weeks to reach your home office. So if you decide that buying supplies by mail order is the way you want to go be sure that you order far enough in advance so that you won't run out. The following is a listing of some mail order firms which supply stationery items and other consumables such as ribbons and printing cartridges. This list is by no  means exhaustive, and by placing a company on this list we are not saying that they are the best in the world either. There are companies not on this list that may be better. The list is merely intended as a starting point for you.

STATIONERY HOUSE INC.
1000 FLORIDA AVENUE
HAGERSTOWN, MD 21741
1-800-638-3033

ROLLAND BUSINESS SUPPLY
500 MAIN STREET
GROTTON, MA 01471
1-800-225-9550

PENNY-WISE
4350 KENILWORTH AVENUE
EDMONSTON, MD 20781
1-800-942-3311

GRAPHICS SUPPLY COMPANY
1612 CALIFORNIA STREET
OMAHA, NE 68101
1-800-228-7272

FIDELITY PRODUCTS COMPANY
P.O. BOX 155
MINNEAPOLIS, MN 55440
1-800-328-3034

DINKLES
P.O. BOX 160
NEWTOWN, MA 02195
1-800-333-3330

BELL ATLANTIC SUPPLIES
456 CREAMERY WAY
EXTON, PA 19341
1-800-523-0552

MOORE BUSINESS PRODUCTS
P.O. BOX 5000
VERNON HILLS, IL 60061
1-800-323-6230

Those companies should be enough to get you started. In fact, once you get on a few mailing lists, even through minor purchases, you will be receiving more catalogs than you can imagine! It's a great way to comparison shop, without ever leaving home. My strong recommendation is to look in your local telephone directory and visit your local stationery store. You may be pleasantly surprised to learn that your local businessman will compete very effectively for your business. Just remember, never overbuy, only buy what you need, when you need it.

CHAPTER 5

ADVERTISING AND MARKETING

YOU MEAN I HAVE TO PAY FOR ADVERTISING TOO!

Now that you have all this wonderful equipment and supplies tucked away in your basement, den, or part of your living room you might expect people to come and ring your bell without telling them you are there, and that you are in business. They won't! *You* will have to contact *them.* You must advertise. Many home based entrepreneurs, who do everything else right, never advertise, or advertise so little and so infrequently, they may as well not bother. Think of what is going on. You selected most of the things you have purchased, and most of the services you use because of advertising. Why should your business be any different?

Advertising can seem to be expensive. But it is a fact of business life that the more advertising, and the better advertising that you do, the more business you *will* get. One thing that you should do first before you advertise is to install a second telephone number in your house, for the exclusive use of your business. This will make things a lot easier for your customers. It will also allow you to advertise your telephone number without having to tie up your home phone and give your private number to strangers. Remember, *keep the kids off the business line,* and be sure that they don't answer it— ever! Buy an answering machine, in fact, buy a two line answering machine and it'll take care of your private number also.

In addition you should give your business a name even if it is only something like Joe Smith's Typing Service.[1] The phone company takes a dim view of you answering your telephone, that is your private telephone, with a business name. You should name this second number in the name of your company to get you a listing in your local telephone directory Yellow Pages—itself a great advertisement.

INEXPENSIVE ADVERTISING

There are a number of inexpensive ways which you can advertise. If you have business cards made up by your local printer you should not only have your name and telephone number on them, but the card should also say that you are in the word processing and typing business. Put these cards on bulletin boards in local supermarkets and the community bulletin boards in your area. This type of advertising can be effective, and the cost is only that of having a few hundred business cards printed.

Another good, inexpensive, ad that you can run is a small classified ad under word processing or typing in your local "buyers" newspaper. For less than twenty dollars an issue of that paper you can have your ad in the home's of everyone in your area. It has been our experience that this ad has been very effective, particularly during the start up of your business. Remember, to not be discouraged if you get no phone calls or customers after the first couple of weeks that the ad has been running. It generally takes months for advertising to have an effect.

Your ad maybe noticed by many people but they will not call you until they have something they need to be typed. They will remember seeing your ad in that local buyers paper when they have

---

1 Remember to register this fictitious name with your State. They will check to be sure that the name is not being used by another company. If you use your name as the company name, the likelyhood of it being used is minimal.

something that needs to be typed and they will go to that paper and find someone that can offer that service.

Therefore your ad should appear every time that paper comes out. If you look through your edition of your local buyers paper you will find there are several companies that are there all the time, you will also find typing service classified ads that come and go. The people that only run an ad occasionally are only cheating themselves on that hit and miss approach will work only if you are very lucky. But when you start looking at these papers look at the number of people whose ad is there all the time. They are not spending that money if they are getting no results. Remember that in order for you to get the same sort of results you must run your ad for some time (at least 6 month).

YELLOW PAGES

If you have invested in a second phone number for your business you will have a one line listing in both the white pages and the yellow pages of your local directory. In a year or so as your business

begins to grow you may want to think of placing a display ad, or at least a bold face ad, in your local Yellow Pages. This is somewhat expensive, and this is the reason we are suggesting that you hold off placing the yellow pages ad until the business has been established for at least a year. Advertising in the phone book becomes expensive because of the number of places you could possibly list your business. For example:

- *Word Processing Service*
- *Typing Service*
- *Resume Service*
- *Mail List Preparation*

Ideally, you should be listed in all those sections, assuming you offer all the services, because there is no way to tell how someone will look it up. The cost for simple listings in all those sections could be over $100 per month. That's a lot of money for your business, and that's just one book![2]

It is probably safe to wait a year before actually placing an ad in the Yellow Pages. For the first time, pick one heading like "Word Processing" and run a small display ad, with a listing under one other section, like "Typing Service." This should cost about $50 to $75 per month. Keep track of the ad's effectiveness for the next year, if it brings in more money in sales than your paying for the ad, keep it. If not, drop it.

Having an ad in the Yellow Pages directory is very effective. People tend to use the Yellow Pages in order to find business like yours that are not generally found in shopping centers. Finally, at the risk of having R.H. Donnelly angry with me, stick with Bell. Our experience says people use the Bell Yellow Pages more.

CHAMBER OF COMMERCE

You may also consider joining your local Chamber of Commerce. This group which meets on some regular basis, lets you come in contact with other people who are running small businesses. These people may present a good source of potential customers for your typing service.

DIRECT MAIL ADS

Direct advertising is sending a flyer or brochure to potential customers soliciting their business. This is usually done by mail. Depending on the nature of your typing business, and as the result of some experiments we have conducted in advertising typing services by direct mail, we would not recommend this as an approach.

---

2 Remember there are now two. Your Bell Yellow Pages and the Donnelly Directory.

The problem with using this type of approach is that many people don't think about using a typing service unless they need one at the current moment. If you are sending an advertisement to local small businesses and you are expecting them to respond at the time they receive the mailing, you are probably asking too much. They may not require your services at the time they receive the mailing and certainly nobody keeps "junk mail." So when they do find themselves in the position to require some type of mail list prepared they will probably go to something like a local buyers newspaper or the yellow pages. Spend your ad dollars on these rather than direct mail.

HOW FAR AWAY DO I ADVERTISE?

You can answer this question very simply, and only *you* can answer it. Depending on where in the country you live, you will be able to gage how far people are willing to travel to have something done. You are wasting your adver-

tising if you go beyond this area. Use yourself as a guide. Would you be willing to travel more then 10 or 15 minutes to get a letter typed? Or would you even be willing to travel that long? Whatever answer you come up with may be the effective range of your business. In New York City, it's  doubtful whether anyone would travel more than a few city blocks. In more rural areas, people may accept up to a 20 minute drive, simply because there is no other choice. There will always be exceptions, depending on the type of services that you offer, if the services are unique people will tend to travel further to come to you.

Normally however people tend to come to you if you are convenient, they will go to your competitor all other things being equal if your competitor happens to be just a few minutes away and you are a ten minute drive. Remember that you can overcome this obstacle to home base word processing business by offering better and different products then can generally be found in a word processing business. Pricing, that is, how much you charge for a given product will also affect how far people are willing to come for your services.[3]

Some Examples

Here are some examples of word processing ads which have been effective over time. They are from a local Yellow Pages, and a local buyer's newspaper. Use these as models, but be comfortable with what you say. Say it in you own language and make sure the things you offer are things that you can do really well.

TYPING SERVICE

DIAMONDE ENTERPRISES
 Serving South Jersey Voorhees 346-9242
LOR PERSONNEL DIVISION
 418 Wall St Princeton 921-6580
M J L TYPING-EDITING
 15 Bratman Dr Hamilton 888-0823
ON-WORD
 Fast Reliable Word Processing Services At
 A Reasonable Rate   Termpapers-Resumes
 Letters-Envelopes   Mailing-Manuscripts
 Form Letters   Over 10 Years
 Academic, Legal And Medical Experience
 11 George Washington Dr
Titusville .... **(609) 737-1720**
SUPREME TYPING Hamilton Township 581-0605
WORD PROCESSING SERVICENTER THE
 795 Parkway Av Trenton 883-1859

One final thought Remember it is very easy to over-spend on advertising, but it is also much easier t o under

TYPING

A PLUS RESUMES — desktop publishing, word processing, etc. 345-1414.

ALL-TYPE TYPING — Confidential, quick, reasonable. 25 years experience. 543-5891.

MASTER KEYS — Let us help you with your typing needs. Fast, accurate and dependable. Call 215-547-5710.

WORD PROCESSING — Laser print. Letters, reports, flyers, microtape transcriptions. Desktop publishing. Low rates. Fast service. Free disk storage. Resumes from $5. Visa/Mastercard accepted.

---

3 There is one other factor. Many people will not use your service because you are "home based." Get used to it. A few of the smart one's will figure out that you can charge less for top quality service because you have less overhead.

spend. In order to elevate you word processing service to something higher then a hobby it will be necessary that you spend on advertising. *Advertising must be honest*, and it must be consistently found in one place every time. When your new customer comes looking for you, you'd better be there. It will do you no good if you advertise a few weeks, stop for a few months, and then advertise for a few weeks more. Once you find the best place for you to advertise in your area, and it will probably be the local buyers newspaper, then place your ad and let it run continuously.

When people come to you, ask them how they heard about your business. This is an important way for you to track the effectiveness of your advertising. Keep track of how many people an ad brings in each month, and more importantly keep track of how many dollars the ad brings in.[4] If after five or six months the number of dollars an ad brings in is less then the cost of the ad you maybe advertising in the wrong place. If you feel you are advertising in the right spot it, may be that it is the ad that's not attracting potential

buyers. At that point try rewriting the ad and running it again, but remember it will take a minimum of four to six months before you can tell whether an ad has been effective or not. But do advertise, somewhere. Remember if you don't advertise *somewhere* you will not get any customers.

Marketing

Advertising is, of course, only part of an overall group of things which one can do to make filling a customers wants and needs a bit easier. This overall group of things is called *marketing*. Advertising was mentioned first because in the establishment of a home based typing or word processing service you can place an effective ad in your local newletter or yellow pages simply by looking at your competitions copy and using it as a guide to write your own ad. Never be afraid to copy from successful, perhaps larger competitors. If you place your ads as soon as you are ready to begin business, (actually a few weeks before) you will begin

---

4 If you are running more than one ad, track each independently.

generating sales and will be able to begin a marketing program which may change these ads at a later date.

Marketing consists of several things you should do

to learn who your customers are,

to know what your customers want and need,

and learn how to reach these customers, so they know you have what they want at a "good" price.

There are five major points that are normally considered in marketing:

• *Who are your customers?*

• *What is your product?*

• *How much should you charge?*

• *How do you get your product to your customer?*

• *How do you best advertise and sell that product?*

WHO IS THE CUSTOMER?

After you get started with your business, you should keep track of the type of people who use your service. From this kind of simple record keeping, you can learn at whom to target your ads and selling, what kinds of services they are most interested in, and even get an idea of whether your pricing is appropriate.

In your home based typing service, you will likely find that your customers fall into three categories:

• *individuals*

• *small business owners*

• *larger corporations*

Naturally, all you customers are *people* regardless of whether they are representing themselves or General Motors. But categorizing the people who become your customers, by the type of company they represent (if any), where they come from, how much money they spend, etc., will help you and your business. This kind of activity results in inforamtion which is called *demographics*.

Larger companies may study such things as customers' income and how these people spend their money on a variety of purchases. These companies also study differences in cultural background, psychological behavior, and how a customer decides to make a purchase. Such studies are expensive and time consuming. It is likely that you will neither be able to afford the time nor the money for such a study. But there are a few inexpensive things that you can do to determine what kinds of people are out there in your market area.

Besides chatting with your customers (and your competitors) to find out what they want and need, browse through your local Yellow Pages. Drive through any local office parks. From what you see and read, you will be able to determine, for example, if there are a lot of small to medium sized businessess in your area, compared with larger companies.

If you find that there are many small businesses, that is, businesses with only a few employees, then you will want to offer services which will appeal to *them*. These things might include business letters, reports, mail lists, proposals, and some simple (complicated analysis, if you know how to do it) spreadsheet analysis. You should offer those things which would give these small business people the advantage of having a

secretary, and the things that a secretary does, without the need for them to hire one (or another one) until they can afford to do so.

If the businesses in your area are large, that is, they have hundreds of employees—including typists, then to get business from them you will need to offer "overflow" services. You will need to offer speed and pricing which will offset the cost of overtime during a period when their work must be ready "yesterday."

Many of your individual customers—those representing themselves —will be interested in an occasional letter, but most will probably be interested in resumes and school reports, ranging from a simple composition, to a Ph.D. thesis.

From your demographic studies, that is knowing what kinds of people are around, you may be able to offer to different kinds of resumes—at two different prices.[5] A normal typeface resume, at a low price, may be all an hourly worker may need, or an out of work person can afford. "Typeset" resumes,

---

5 This also assumes you have the appropriate software and printers.

at a higher price, may be needed by professional and managerial customers, or by those who only want the best.

Just remember that the more you learn about your customers, the more you will be able to give them what they want.

WHAT IS THE PRODUCT?

The basic product that you will offer in your home based word processing business is the "typed" page. Depending on the equipment and the software that you have, this page may take many different forms. The products you offer will also grow as the business and your investment grows.

The following is a list of the possible products you can offer. The list is not meant to be all inclusive, neither is it meant to show the products you must offer to start your business.

PRODUCTS

- *Double Spaced Pages*
  - *Photocopies*
  - *Statistical Typing*
  - *Business Letters*
- *Envelopes, addressed*
  - *Resumes*

- *Manuscripts*
  - *Reports*
- *Thesis, and term papers*
  - *Mail lables*
- *Multiple address letters*
  - *Mail lists*
- *Text typesetting and page layout*
- *Posters, flyers, overheads*
  - *Forms*
  - *Graphs*

These are some of the different forms your "typed" page may take. Of course, to offer some of them, you will have to have the equipment, such as a photocopy machine, or the specialized software to produce the product. All these need not be offered when

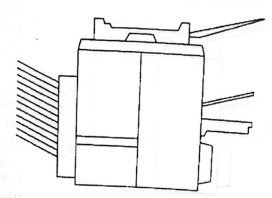

you begin. At the beginning, you should offer at least the following basic services:

- *Double & single spaced pages*
  - *Addressed envelopes*
    - *Business letters*
      - *Mail lists*
      - *Resumes*
      - *Reports*
      - *Thesis*

New products can be added later, when you've made some money and want to invest further in your business. In fact, adding new products is probably a good time to remind all your old customers that your still there, as you tell them about your new product. It's also a good time to give them a new price list with any price increases you may need to make.

In time, you may want to offer things like GBC© bindings, those plastic spiral bindings, a dictation service, and a fax service. These extra services are not necessary, but remember, the more you offer a customer, the more convenient you make it for that customer. The better the quality of your work, the more likely it is that the customer will return—and perhaps become dependent on your service, thus insuring your future profits!

HOW MUCH DO YOU CHARGE?

The question of how much to charge is not easily answered in general terms. It depends on where you live. Your pricing should flow from the price you charge for the basic typed page, that is, the double-spaced page. If you live near a big city you may find that others are charging up to $3.00 for a d.s. page. Others may be charging as low as $1.00. You must look at what the competitors in your area are charging. If you determine that you cannot make money at that price, or you feel you product will be better then you should price higher. If you feel they have been charging to much, and you can make a reaonable profit at a lower price then price your product lower.

Assuume that $1.75 is reasonable for a double spaced page, (That's $3.50 for a single spaced page—it's the same price. Think about it!) then your resume pages may be $5.00 to $10.00 per page. Statistical typing might be $4.50 per page.

Finally, include an OFF HOUR Service charge and a SAME DAY Service charge on your price list. These will keep cutomers in line who will take advantage of the fact that your business is home based and that you are always there. Add a $20.00 surcharge for all work done on Holidays, and weekends, and a 50% extra charge for work that must be returned the same day. This way only those who really need the work are likely to insist on it. Remember if things are not busy, you can always waive the same day charge, or work Saturday for that good customer! The next chapter will cover pricing in detail.

HOW DO YOU GET YOUR PRODUCT TO YOUR CUSTOMER?

Getting the product to the customer is known as *distribution*. In the case of the home based typing/word processing service, the delivery of the product to the customer is simple. For the most part, you have only one choice. *The customer must come to you to deliver and pick up the work.* As you might expect, you will have to pay for this simplicity. Depending on where your home, and therefore your place of business, is located, the fact that the customer will have to visit you *twice* will limit your business. Most customers expect this and will therefore look for lower prices than a secretarial service that delivers. Others will refuse to do business with you when they find you are home based. Keep your pricing high enough to make a profit and *don't apologize* for not delivering. For the most part, if you treat the situation as normal, your customers will also.

If you have, or can afford a fax machine, you can cut the number of trips that your customer has to make. They can fax you the work to be done, and you can return the finished work by fax so they can proofread 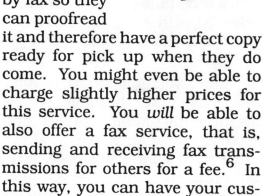 it and therefore have a perfect copy ready for pick up when they do come. You might even be able to charge slightly higher prices for this service. You *will* be able to also offer a fax service, that is, sending and receiving fax transmissions for others for a fee.[6] In this way, you can have your customers help pay for your fax machine.

---

6 Prices vary. Check the prices charged by others in your area.

PICK UP AND DELIVERY

Someday, if your business grows sufficiently, you may want to consider a pick up and delivery service. You will of course need more employees than yourself to make this work. If at some point you feel that this service will help your business grow, then you will have to decide whether it will be free —say within a 10 mile radius—and what you will charge beyond this "home" base.

This service will likely cause an increase in all your prices, and it is justified as you are offering a convenience. Also important, is that you set a schedule. For example, you may tell your customers that the service is available by calling the day before. You will make all work pick ups between 9:00 AM and 10:30 AM. Finished work will be returned between 3:30 PM and 5:00 PM, *on the day you tell them the work will be done.* In this way you won't be running around every ten minutes when someone decides their letter is ready. You can also charge extra for emergency pick up on demand. Just make the charge high enough to discourage people from taking advantage of it, and you.

SELLING AND ADVERTISING

Besides the things we mentioned at the beginning of this chapter, remember your best ad, and your best salesperson is a *satisfied customer.* Never underestimate the power of "word of mouth." Customers will either make or break you. If someone asks Joe where he got his resume done and he says: "Go to Acme Typing over on 4th Street in the blue house. It's great!" You have a new customer. If Joe says: " I can tell you where not to go...stay away from Acme." Guess what happens—and *word will get around.*

Chapter 6

PRICING

Business people will tend to tell you less about how they arrived at pricing of their products than about almost any other part of their business. Unless they happen to be in well regulated businesses, they will very rarely tell you how they arrived at the price of the product.

In the case of your home based typing business setting a price should not be too much of a problem, at the beginning. It should generally be about the same as what other home based word processing services are charging in your area. Remember that no customer in his right mind would pay more to you for the *same* service he can get for less from someone else. Because of this you can see why keeping your operating costs low is very important.

In addition there is a psychological expectation on the part of your customers. Because your business is home based they will expect to pay less then they would pay for the same service from a business which is established in a store front building. In fact, you will find that some people will not do business with you at all, once they find you are working from home.[1]

However, at some point, you may find that in your local area the services and the quality you can provide are some what *better than* can be had from most others. Listen to your customers' comments, you'll learn if your better. In this case you may want to charge slightly more for your product. You might even get it. You may even want to take an opposite tactic. If you know your product is better, you may want to charge the same or slightly *less* if your cost will allow it and thereby "buy" your way into a market segment of word processing in your local area.[2]

COST PLUS PRICING

One of the easiest ways to set your price is a matter of simple arithmetic, or *pricing on a cost plus basis.* Even if you don't set your prices on this basis, knowing your costs is important because you will not be able to survive unless you bring more money in, than you pay out. You set your price in this way by taking your cost for a given product and adding to it some number representing a *fair profit.*[3]

If it turns out that in one of the products that you are offering your costs *exceed* the price you can sell the product for you have no choice but to raise the selling price of that product. You can

---

1 This may be because some of them have had bad experiences with home typists, like poor quality and lack of dependability. It could be that they're just snobs.
2 In the world of big business, the Japanese are experts at buying market share. They are patient enough to operate for years—at a loss if necessary— in order to capture a major share of a market. In the US, most managers and shareholders are too concerned with current earnings to think about the future.
3 What's a fair profit? Some would say whatever you can get, as things are determined by supply and demand. Others would say around 30% for a commodity and 100+% for a specialty item.

raise the price to the point where it equals cost so that you break even on each item sold and not lose money. In some cases you may *have* to do this because of competitive pricing and because despite your costs, you cannot afford *not* to sell a given product. The only thing you can do in this latter case is to raise the price to the point where it is exactly equal to your costs and make no money on it. In this way you will be able to gain a customer and make money on other products while essentially be offering this as a free service.[4] The alternative to this is, if you don't offer it as a service because you cannot compete, *you may lose the customer to one of your competitors.*

Let's try a simple example of cost plus pricing. We will price a typed double spaced page. First let's establish cost:

COST PLUS CALCULATION

Paper (1 ream @ $20.00) =
$20/500 pgs = $0.04 per page

Ribbon (1 ribbon @$15.00
1,500 pages per ribbon)=
$15/1500 pages = $0.01 per page

Your time ($25.00 per hour
& typing 80 wpm & 200 words per pg.)
= $25/60min/80wpm x 200 wds/pg. =

$1.04 per page

TOTAL COST = $ 1.09 per d.s. page
(not including electric costs!)

Now that you have your cost you can calculate *the price* you will charge by adding on a profit:
at 10% profit the price will be $1.20
at 20% profit the price will be $1.31
at 40% profit the price will be $1.53
at 50% profit the price will be $1.64
at 60% profit the price will be $1.75

What is a reasonable price in this case? It depends. Profit margins in excess of 40% for this sort of critical service are not unusual. But if all the exisitng businesses in your area are charging $1.25 per page, you can expect few customers if you charge $ 1.75, unless you have something else to offer. You can also see, from these calculations, how the cost of your materials is important. If you buy your paper correctly you can reduce your direct expense (i.e., money spent out of pocket) to perhaps $0.01 per page—or less!

You could also calculate your hourly labor rate at less than $25.00. After all, you could get only $8.00 an hour working part time at the local supermarket. That would lower costs a great deal. Remember these things:

4   Don't let your customer know it's "free".

you will determine your "salary"

you will not get overtime for the hours you work

you will pay for any benefits you may have to get (this cost some companies an additional 25% of salary or more)

you are in business to make a profit

Perhaps, in your section of the country, $25 is high (or low), if so, adjust the number. Whatever number you use for your time, *never undervalue yourself!*[5]

To help establish whether your prices are correct, I will show you how to get the information you may need to check these prices in the following sections. Now, you should ask yourself some questions.

If your prices are higher than your competitors ask yourself the question is the product, the quality of the products I am selling better than my competitors?

Regardless of how your prices compare to your competitors ask yourself the question: How will your competitors react to the pricing you set? Will they cut prices to meet yours, if you've lowered the prices? Will they improve their products, or will they offer better service and newer products to counteract your presence?

TAKE A CLOSE LOOK AT YOUR COMPETITORS

One of the things you should do immediately (as soon as you need a break in reading) is to go through your local phone book, and newspaper and get the phone numbers of people who are advertising that are in home based word processing businesses.

---

5 People have a strange reaction if the price of something is much lower than they expect to pay, many of them assume that their is something wrong with the product. Sometimes they're right.

Also, get the names of some of the word processing businesses that may operate out of shopping centers or office buildings. Call them up and ask them their prices for typing various types of documents such as: letters, resumes, reports and mail lists. This way, in a day or two, you'll be able to come up with a list of what is being charged by your competitors. You don't have to tell them *why* you want the pricing, or that you are starting a new business and you would like to check out what they are doing. You don't have to feel bad about doing it, either. Most people will be happy to give you their pricing; they will assume that you are a potential customer.

Once you have this information, you can analyze it, by showing the range of pricing from the lowest price to the highest price and then calculating a simple average. From each of these three costs, low, average, and high, you should subtract your cost, which you can calculate from the money you've spent for your supplies. You can then calculate how much of a profit you would make at each price level. Don't forget to allow for a profit in the time you invested in preparing the document (your hourly labor rate).

If your costs are below all these prices you are in relatively good shape. If you follow some of the guidelines we've given in previous chapters your costs *should* be low enough to enable you to compete at any level. If you can *honestly* answer that the quality of material that you give customers is much better than anyone else in the area then you maybe justified in charging on the higher end of the price range.

But remember that if you are starting out no one will know how good you are, so you may want to start your pricing at the lower end and work up to the higher prices, when your reputation as an extremely high quality word processor becomes common knowledge. It would be better at the start for your business, if your prices are either slightly below or at the average range of your competitors.

Prices are not fixed in stone and can always be changed later. In fact, the prices *will* have to be changed, as cost of materials go up, or as your reputation gets better.

THE PRICE OF A PAGE

Pricing for word processing services begins with the fundamental price for a normal typed written page. You may choose this typed written page to come out on an average typed written document if it was double spaced. The price of this double spaced page is your foundation price.

In order to check the kind of price which will be acceptable for your region of the country, we would suggest that you go to your local newsstand and buy the current edition of *Writers Digest*. In the classified section of this magazine you will find "yellow pages" of classified ads for typing manuscript pages for aspiring writers. Each one of these ads is grouped by state and generally gives the price of a typed double spaced page.

Find your state or city and look at the pricing in these ads and that will help determine your basic price per page. You will note that these prices range from $1.00 per double spaced page to sometimes as high as $3.00-3.50 per double

spaced page. Remember that all your pricing is done per piece according to *your output*. If your customer gives you a hand written document, and writes very small, what they write on three pages may come out to four or five doubles spaced pages. *You bill them according to your output not what they give you.*

THE PRICE LIST

Once you have the basic price for a double space page, you can go on and price other products based on this. Look closely at the price list given here, and you will see that once the document is in the computer and you have charged, for example $1.75, for the double spaced page that you have previously completed, if the customer wants an additional copy, an additional " original "

copy, from the printer you can then charge less. In this example only $1.00 per page.

Price List

Basic Rate ....$1.75 per ds page
Original Copies........$1.00 per page
Photocopies ....$0.15 per copy
Statistical typeing....$4.50 per page
Business Letter ....$2.25 per page
Addressed envelope .$0.50 each
with letter................$0.15 each
Changes ....$1.00 per page
Resume ....$5.00 per page
Resume typeset or prep
...............................$30.00 minimum
Multi address letter or
mail labels...............$1.00 setup/10
plus.........................$1.00 per letter or
...............................$0.10 per label
Poster/Flyer ....$10.00 per page
GBC© Binding.........$2.50 each
Line Drawing...........$25.00 each
Form Creation ....$25.00 per page
Off hour charge $20.00
Same Day service ....add 50%

Also note that some things have a higher price, for example, statistical typing, which is the preparation of large numeric tables, or columns of words. These require much more work and should be charged accordingly— higher. As shown in this example statistical typing is charged at $4.50 per output page.

You can also see from this example that business letters are charged at a much higher apparent price than the basic rate. Actually it's less. The reason behind this is that business letters tend to be only one page long and are single spaced, it would then simply not be worth your time to type a single business letter for $1.75. In addition, customers would find $3.50 (the single spaced page charge, and the correct logical charge) too high for a simple letter. So the price is raised, as in this example, to $2.25, between the single and double spaced page rates—neither you nor the customer get cheated.

Remember one thing. The charge of $1.75 per double space page is the basic rate. This means that if your customer wishes the output to be in a single spaced page, then the price that you charge for a single spaced page is $3.50 or exactly twice the price of a double spaced page.

At first, some customers maybe upset by this sort of pricing. Be patient and explain to them that $1.75 per double spaced page is exactly the same price as $3.50 per single spaced page. This is because with the output of the single spaced page, they will get approximately double the amount of words and therefore the amount of pages they pay for are approximately half. The total price they have been charged is the same. As noted, business letters are not charged at a single spaced page rate of $3.50, but are reduced because business letters are usually relatively short.

There are other prices shown on the example list. Some of them are dependent upon the availability of your business having certain computer programs. As was mentioned before, having graphics and desktop page layout programs will allow you to do such things as drawings, data graphs, posters and the creation of forms. These more complicated documentsThey are often products not found in many home based typing services. are accordingly priced higher.

One price that you should note is the price for resumes. In this price list, the cost for typing a simple resume, when the customer knows how they want it formatted, and you are merely typing, is $5.00 per page. In many areas of the country, resumes are charged much higher, even $30.00-40.00 for a simple resume typed. This is one advantage you can use over your competitors. For no conceivable reason, if you are merely typing someone's resume should you have to charge $30.00-40.00! It is just like typing any other document. *Advertise low price resumes.* The advantage in this lies in the fact that many people who *need* a resume are out of work

and can not afford the $30.00-40.00, *but they need a resume.* They will be able to afford a charge of $5.00 per page and be very pleased, particularly if the quality

of the resume you give them is very good. The disadvantage of such a low price compared with what others charge for resumes, is the problem we have mentioned that some people will wonder why, and assume the quality is no good. Hang in there with this one, it'll eventually work.

Also notice a second resume charge on the example price list. The charge of $30.00 minimum is for *preparing*[6] the resume or for laying it out on a desktop publishing program, and providing a laser "typeset" document. An example of a "regular" and a "typeset" resume is given in Appendix 3.

6 Assuming you know how.

HOURS AND AVAILABILITY

Because you work at home, the service you will be able to offer and in fact, *you must really offer*, is for customers to drop off their work in the evening.[7] Most of your customers work full time, and will not be able to drop off their work during the normal 9 to 5 business hours. So you must be able to allow them to drop off and pick up their work after 5 or at some other reasonable hour.

Because of this, and because you are working out of your home, this will give them the impression that you will be there to do what they want *at any time*. Note on the example price list, there are two additional charges which may be used to discourage abuse in this area. One is an *off hour service charge* which you can use if your customer gives you a 50 page document on a Friday night and tells you they need it on Sunday. Because you are working on the weekend you should charge them more. If their crisis is real they will have no trouble paying the in-

creased charge, if the crisis is not real you will be training them to come to you at more normal hours. The same sort of reasoning holds for the *same day service charge.*

If a customer brings something to you at 8 or 9 in the morning and says that they need it that night *charge extra*. In the case of

the example price list, the charge is 50% extra, using the same day surcharge in this case. If you have very little else to do that day,[8] then you may not want to charge the customer the same day surcharge. If a big part of the reason for this charge is to be sure that the customers are not taking advantage of you don't take advantage of them either. If you have to rearrange the work of other customers to accommodate someone who needs something in a rush then by all means charge extra. If you don't—don't charge!

---

7 or early in the morning
8 It may happen during the first few months, and probably during certain months as the business tends to be seasonal.

THE SMALL PRINT

Let's take a look at some notes which you may want on the bottom of the price list. These are just friendly little reminders to your customers as to things which they might already know, but things about which you don't want any misunderstanding.

Notes

Payment is expected in full on completion. Make checks payable to Acme Typing Service (or your name). Book length manuscripts, term papers, and thesis require 1/2 payment at the start and the remaining 1/2 on completion. Rates subject to change without notice. Errors/changes made by customer will incur additional charges. Always keep a copy of any work you submit. $10.00 fee for returned checks. We are not liable for any direct, consequential, or incidental loss or damage.

As you can see your customers should expect to pay you in full at the completion of the work. They really should not get their work unless they'd paid for it. The exceptions to this are, of course, people you know well and can trust, and long standing good customers. Also note that longer documents such as book manuscripts, term papers, and thesis would require half payment before the work begins. The other half payment can be made when the work is complete. This is done for your own protection. If you spent your time and money typing a 50 page term paper for a student, or a 400 page book manuscript for an aspiring novelist, and for one

reason or another they lose interest and do not return, you are out quite a bit of money. If you receive half the payment up front on these longer documents and the customer never returns that advance payment should more than cover your costs.

The other notes are self-explanatory.

HOW CAN YOU TELL IF YOU ARE MAKING MONEY?

The most important thing that you have to keep track of is *cash flow*. Cash flow is exactly what it sounds like. It is the flow of money in and out of your business.

The cash flow is said to be *positive* if there is more money coming into the business then is going

out, that is, if you are making more money then you are spending.

The cash flow is *negative* if you are spending more money then you are making.

For the first eight or twelve months of your business expect a negative cash flow.[9] The reason for this is simple, during this initial start up period you will be spending a great deal of money on equipment and supplies in order to get your business started. At the same time, you generally won't have a large number of customers. As time goes on however, things should change. The number of customers should increase and the amount of cash that you have to pay for supplies should naturally go down. At this point your cash flow should go from a negative to a positive number. *Maintaining a positive cash flow is the most important aspect of your business.*

GROSS MARGIN

You may have heard of people talking about *gross margin*, that is, the difference between the selling price and the actual cost of a product expressed as a percent. Your gross margin should be relatively high, if you have purchased your supplies and equipment correctly. However, the gross margin does not necessarily put money in the bank. *You can still have a high*

---

9 If there are no other typing services around, you may get lucky and start to make a profit even sooner.

gross margin with a negative cash flow. The one financial indicator that you should watch constantly, and always, is the *cash flow.*

If the cash flow remains negative there is one simple question that you should ask yourself and answer. *Am I spending too much money for the level of business that I have?*

If the answer is yes, and the things you are spending money on are *not necessary* for the growth of your business, that is, things like a brand new desk, fancy lamps, etc. stop spending! If the things you are spending are important for the growth of the business that is, advertising, flyers and things of that sort you should give them a chance to work, before deciding to drop them.

If however expensive advertising is not bringing in customers after three or four months then abandon the advertising and try something different.

The simplest way to keep track of cash flow is to simply to keep track of the amount of money that you've made. Track the dollar sales that you have made for a given period, whether it be a week or a month, and how much money you have spent on expenses for your business during that same

period (Remember the budget table). If you subtract the expenses from the dollar amount that you've made, and the number is a positive number, then the business is going well. If negative, reassess what you are doing.

When you are about to spend any amount of money on your business take a look at the affect of that expenditure on your cash flow. If the cash flow remains positive, then you can make the expenditure. If the purchase makes the cash flow negative, or more negative, then ask yourself the question is this expense necessary for the growth of the business. If the answer is yes and you can afford it, then go ahead and make the purchase. If the answer is no do *not* make the purchase. Remember the only important thing for your small business is whether there is more cash coming in or going out.

If you've answered the question: "Am I spending too much money for the level of business that I have?" with an honest "No!" then you may have to decide whether you should stay in the business.

This is one of the toughest decisions anyone in business ever has to make. It's tough even for Vice Presidents of big businesses who have to decide whether to continue a project or not. People generally do not admit failure easily.

If you determine that you're not overspending, and you have been doing some advertising so that people know you're in business, and you still have a negative cash flow after a year or so, you may *not* have a business.[10] This sad state of affairs may not be your fault.[11] It may be that you live in a section of the country where there aren't enough people to generate the work. It may be that there are so many other word processing services that were in existance before you started, that the newest—you—cannot make your niche in the marketplace. Try to find out the reason. Whatever the reason turns out to be, stop pouring money into a bottomless hole. Stop for a while, see if you can come up with a way to change things. If not, move on. Try a new business.

There is such a thing as "failing your way to sucess". If having your own business is truly something you want, don't give up. Keep trying. Try the same business again with a different twist, try some other venture. There are many things for which you can use your computer. Start a computer *billboard*, a data retrieval service in a specific area, train people to use computers, or write a book! The point is to do something, preferably something you like. Many business people do not have successful businesses until the third or fourth try! Everytime you fail, you learn something. If you learn enough things not to do, and don't do them, sooner or later you will be successful. But remember, success will never come to someone who has given up.

CHANGING PRICES

Changing prices, especially when you have to *raise* them is always a problem. This is true even though we all expect things to always go up! At some point in the life of your home based word

---

10 If you have sales in exces of $7,000 or 8,000 at this time, with a negative cash flow, check your answer about spending.
11 It is, if you've done lousy work and no one ever comes back!

CHAPTER SIX

processing business, you will probably have to raise the price on some of your products. Prices will have to be increased for all or some of the following reasons:

- *Pricing was wrong in the first place*
- *Costs of materials have gone up*
- *Operating costs have gone up (electricity, etc.)*
- *You want to increase profits*

If your materials costs, or operating costs have gone up, you may have to increase the prices of all your products to maintain your profitability. If you've mispriced only one item or two then change just them.

If, for example, you find that you're the only one in your area offering a certain service you may want to increase the price on that service simply because you have no competitors. If you're the only act in town, take advantage of it.[12]

You may simply decide that you want to increase the profitability of your business by generally increasing your prices by 15%. Whatever the reason you should do these things:

- *Change your price list, and stop using the old list, and*
- *Send this new price list to all your previous customers.*

Unless there is a real emergency, you should not increase your prices more than twice a year. You should also realize that no matter how justified your increases may be, you will loose one or two customers, because of a price increase.

If you can arrange it, one of the best ways to increase the prices of some items would be to *simultaneously decrease* the price of some others.

12It's done all the time. Check the airline fares to places served by only one airline, and compare them to fares thousands of miles away.

If you have some over-priced products, particularly one's that don't sell, try reducing them at the time you raise others. If you have new services to offer, include them in the new price list you send to the customers. These things will help make your price increases easier to take. If you can do neither of these things, but still must increase prices, include a coupon good for 20% OFF, or whatever, to help "sugar coat" a price increase. Just remember to put an expiration time on the offer- say 30 days from the date you send it.

When you send your new price list to your customers, include a cover letter which explains the reasons why you were "forced" to make the increases due to increased cost of paper, or whatever. In this letter, you can then highlight the new services, or the prices that were lowered, or point out the money saving offer.

TRADING AND BARGAINING

Some customers will offer to trade their services for yours. This could be a real advantage if they have something you need. For example, suppose a local independent phone installer will install your business line in exchange for $200 worth of typing, or a local contractor offers to finish your basement if you supply his work free for a year. If it's something you need, and the trade seems fair go ahead and do it.

What happens if a customer asks for a discount? Suppose they say: "I have 65 pages to type and think I should get a break." I would suggest that you should stick with your rates. After all, your in the business of typing pages. Once you start discounting, then, especially with that particular customer, it will be virtually impossible to hold price. The decision to discount is ultimately yours.

CHAPTER 7

WHAT SERVICES DO I OFFER?

BASIC SERVICES

Basic services that you must offer in order to have an on-going home based typing or word processing service are relatively simple ones .

You must be able to provide both double space and single space typed pages. You must be able to provide high quality business letters and addressed envelopes.

Resumes are also an important part of your word processing business. It is not necessary, at the beginning, to provide "typeset" resumes but it is necessary to provide high quality typewritten resumes. If you don't know how to prepare a resume, or are unfamiliar with the basic forms of a resume, I would suggest that you go to your local library and find a book on resume preparation and study it carefully. You will find that your customers expect certain things from a resume. They expect it to look like a resume. They expect *you* to know what a resume looks like, and how to prepare them.

FLYERS AND GRAPHICS

If you own the proper software, (see the section on software), or if you have a sufficient number of requests from potential customers to justify the purchase of such software, you should offer the service of preparation of flyers and graphics.

If you refer to the price list in the previous chapter you will see that these sorts of services can be extremely profitable. They are also an important service to other small businesses in your area. Because of your computer based system, and especially if you have a laser printer, you will be able to provide high quality flyers and brochures which can be used by

other small companies to increase their sales at a very reasonable price. This price is generally much higher per page than a standard typed written page. However, it should be priced significantly *less* than what it would cost someone to go to a traditional typesetter in your area. Be careful when providing this service that you don't imply that you can perform a service that you cannot.

Remember to tell your customers that they will not get color output, and that there are certain type of graphics such as circular and flowing letters that you may not be able to provide, if the program you have purchased can not perform that task. Included below are some of the types, flyers,

brochures and forms you should be able to offer your customers if you have the proper equipment to do so.

TYPE OF FLYERS
- *Sales broadsides*
  - *Coupons*
- *Overhead transparencies*
  - *Bulletins*
  - *Catalogs*
  - *Ads*
- *Price lists*

MAIL LISTS

Mail lists are a very important part of word processing or typing service business. Many small businesses do at least part of their advertising by direct mail.

This means that they send a letter or brochure to many hundreds of customers. If you have the right programs you should be able to provide a service of customer mailing lists. Customers will expect you to be able to produce these mailing lists sorted according to a variety of means. If you have the right program this is easy.

Generally larger mailing lists are sorted according to zip code so that the mailer may take advantage of discounts offered by the Postal Service for presorting the mail.[1] Your customers may want their mailing lists sorted alphabetically or by some sort of a code that they may give you. Remember that a dedicated program for this sort of service is

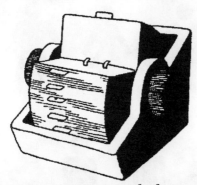

not necessary, provided you have purchased a full featured word processor. At the start up of your business this should be sufficient to provide this service. In addition, a full featured word processor will allow you to provide to your customer more "personalized" form letters using the database of addresses.

As time goes on, and your business picks up it may be beneficial to you to buy a database or mail list program. If the mail list program is compatible with your word processor, or one of your other programs can translate from one to the other, then these types of programs generally make handling bulk mail lists easier for you.

Just remember to price this service low enough so that you don't scare away people with large mailing lists. If you refer to the price list in the previous chapter you may think that ten cents a label is not very profitable. Of course, it doesn't seem very profitable if you are doing a list that is only ten labels long. However, if someone comes to you with a list which may contain 1,500 - 2,000 labels, then a price much higher than 10 or 15 cents per label will scare them off.

MANUSCRIPTS

If you live near a university, or a community college, large manuscripts (200 or 300 pages long) are a good source of business. You may want to have a special rate for these larger manuscripts. The reason for this

1 Contact your local post office to get the brochure, "Third-Class Mail Preparation"

lower special rate is to attract aspiring authors, and students, who probably cannot afford to pay full price for a 500-600 page manuscript.

Graduate school thesis are another important source of profitable business for this type of product. Before you type such a thesis, remember that most graduate school thesis have to be typed precisely, according to a set of rules which may be peculiar to the particular university, or professor that the thesis is being written for. So, to save yourself a lot of aggravation, and to make your customer happy, please be sure that before you start to type such a thesis, your customer has given you all the rules that his or her professor laid down for the preparation of the thesis.

BUSINESS OVERFLOW

Large companies may also be a source of income for your business. Periodically, you should contact large businesses in your area perhaps by letter, or by phone, and let them know of your existence. Let them know of your willingness to do "overflow work " for them.

Overflow work is the result of periodic projects which can happen in a larger company that their secretarial staff cannot handle. It may be cheaper for them to have this extra work done by you than to pay their secretarial staff overtime. It is definitely cheaper than if they have to higher additional people, which they may not really need most of the time. Keep in

mind that many large companies, and some small ones and even some individuals, will try to buy your service at an hourly rate.

Be very careful when or if you do this. What they are generally looking for is to have a large amount of work done for a lower price than you charge on a per page basis. We would suggest, in order to keep your cash flow positive, that you do not advertise an hourly rate. You should however, determine how many letters you type in an hour this should give you a handle on what your hourly rate would be. It should be the same rate—or higher—than the hourly rate you used to compute your costs. When or if business is slow and someone calls and asks you to do some work for them at an hourly rate you will be able to give that charge without hesitation. Remember when you are determining your hourly rate add

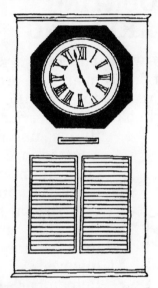

a cushion to your charge because it is unlikely that you will be able to keep up a high rate for several hours.

Example: if you normally charge $2.25 to type a business letter and you determine that you can type 10 such letters in an hour the minimum hourly charge you should quote is $25.00. Now suppose your customer gives you 100 letters; it is unlikely that you will be able to do the 10 letter per hour rate going for 10 hours. In this case you may want to charge a bit more than $25.00 per hour if you think the price you come up with is competitive.

I must mention again, as in a previous chapter, the only way you will know if your price is competitive is to find out what the people in your area charge.

BEYOND THE BASICS

Beyond the basic services just mentioned, are several other things you may want to provide your customers, when your business has grown sufficiently to afford the equipment needed.

For example, you may find, in time, that people will ask you if you do tape transcriptions. In order to do a tape transcription you will have to have a tape transcriber.[2] The cost of the transcriber will range anywhere from $200-500 depending on the type and brand that you buy.

Basically there are three types, one that uses standard cassette tapes. This is the same size used for recording music. There are two smaller size recorders also: the micro-cassette and the mini-cassette. Unfortunately the transcriber will be such that only one size tape will fit. No matter which kind you buy someone will always come with a different size tape. If however you see a pattern of requests for a given size then this is probably the machine that you should invest in. Make sure that the price that you charge for transcription is *exactly* the same as the prices you charge when you get the work given to you in a handwritten format. Remember, however, to tell your customer that in the case of transcription, what they will get, and what they will pay for, is first copy. Since most people dictate in a "draft" form, what you will give them will probably not be what they want for their final copy. They must know that the changes that you make, at their request, after they have seen the hard copy, will be redone at an extra expense to them.

ACCOUNTING - BOOKKEEPING

If and when you own a spreadsheet program and are proficient at its use, you may then offer simple bookkeeping services. The things usually requested are financial summaries of someone's business or a special promotion that a salesman may be involved with. Remember to tell your customer in this case that you are not providing accounting services; you are merely providing simple bookkeeping or formatting data sheets that they have already prepared. If you refer to the price list in the previous chapter, you will see the sort of product is listed

2 If you've never done transcription before, or never done tape transcription, practise before you advertise the service. It's not easy for some people.

under statistical typing. Given proficiency with a spreadsheet program the price charge for this type of service is generally very profitable, and will lead to a positive cash flow.

DESKTOP PUBLISHING

If you own a good desktop publishing program and you have a good laser or a ink jet printer, then you will be able to provide such services as brochures and newsletters. If you refer back to the price list in the previous chapter you will note that there is no price listed for the crea-

ter with, then he would be charged a $1.75 for the initial typing of the double spaced page, and, in addition, you would charge a page charge for setting the text.

Any drawings, data graphs which may be added to the newsletter are charged as individual pieces. Remember, that in order to provide this service you must have a working knowledge of your publishing program, and some feel for design of a page.

There are excellent texts on page design which you may want to refer to at the point where you are willing to provide this service:

tion of a brochure or newsletter. This is because the price you charge is generally a combination of things which are already on the list. For example, if someone gives you a handwritten document to prepare a typical 4 page newslet-

Graphic Design for the Electronic Age by J. D. White

Looking Good in Print by R. C. Parker.

In Appendix 3 are the first page of a typical newsletter and the first page of a restaurant menu. These are typical, profitable services which you can provide with a desktop publishing system.

PICK UP AND DELIVERY

In all probability, potential customers will ask if you will pick up and deliver their work. Whether you do this or not should be based on the simple fact of whether *you can do it or not.*

Generally, if you are working by yourself, it will be very difficult for you to be able to pick up and deliver *and* do the work at the same time. One suggestion would be that if you determine that pick up and delivery is necessary, then you should tell your customers that you will pick up work say between the hours of 8 and 10, and deliver finished work between the hours of 3:30 and 5 for example. This way you will not be running all over town doing pick up and deliveries whenever a customer decides they are ready for you. Pick up and delivery is not a service which is expected from most home based word processing services. You probably don't have to worry about it. However at some point if your business becomes very successful it is a good competitive tool. It is also something you can charge for. You may for example provide free pick up and delivery anywhere within a 5 mile radius and charge something like $5-10 for pick up and delivery beyond that radius. It is a tricky service to offer. Remember, that it should not take time away from your prime business and it should be making you money. Even if you do decide to offer pick up and delivery be sure that you know the real costs. If these costs exceed the amount of sales dollars coming in, then your cash flow will be negative and it is not a service that you should be offering.

CHAPTER 8

BRINGING IT ALL TOGETHER

As you can now see, starting a word processing business in your home is a relatively easy thing to do. Starting a *successful* word processing business, is just as easy, but it requires attention

to some details before you start. It is a relatively inexpensive business to start, that is, it requires only a modest amount of capital to get started. This is particularly true if you already own the equipment which will allow you to enter this business. Because of this

modest *fee for participation*, it is however, generally not a business that will be profitable enough to allow you to retire to a South Sea Island - ever. Contrary to popular thinking, it can offer you a reasonable second income. However it will take a great deal of hard work and some investment perhaps just a bit beyond what you may have expected.

The important thing about such a business and the thing necessary for success is your desire to *want* to be in this type of business. If you would be happier working for yourself, than perhaps as a typist in a pool of a large company, or as a clerk in a local department store, maybe this is the business for you.

If you have decided to be in the business, or if you already are, the most important thing to remember is to keep your cash flow positive. In order to do that there are two very important things you must do.

First, you must let everyone know you are in the business that is you must advertise. Advertising costs money. If your advertising is effective, then it will bring in more money than it costs you. The number of customers and the amount of money they will spend each month will grow.

The second thing that you must remember, in order to keep your cash flow positive, is that you must purchase your supplies and equipment wisely. Refer to other sections in this book in order to begin your purchasing plans. Remember things are generally cheaper if you buy them in packages which contain greater amounts than those generally sold retail packs. Also remember to shop around, bargains can be found almost anywhere. When you see necessary items that are at a special price, and you know the price is good, then make the purchase.

The important thing to remember as you start your home based business is to have fun. If providing these services mentioned in this book are a chore and a drudgery, and you don't look forward to going to work everyday, *then don't do it. You* can make more money and have less aggravation working for someone else. If you enjoy being your own boss, and are not particularly bothered by the uncertainty of your own business, go ahead and do it now. It will be one of the most rewarding things you have ever done in your life.

WORKING WITH YOUR SPOUSE

Suppose you've decided to go all the way with the idea of your own word processing business and both you and your spouse will be working together full time, what then?

I'm sure you've heard of the horror stories about husband and wife working together. Some of the  stories are probably true. If you and your spouse are not really getting along, and don't spend much time together before you start the business, don't expect the business to change anything. If you think being in business together will bring you closer together, you're wrong. If you're not close before you start the business, you won't be after. In fact, it could make an already strained relationship worse. The added stress will not help a poor relationship.

But if you and your spouse are happy, enjoy working with each other, go ahead and do it, no matter what you may have heard. That kind of a partnership can be unbeatable. It has one great benefit no other partnership has, you are with someone who cares...you're not so alone. I know, my husband and I have worked together everyday for years. Sure, we argue, we disagree, but we work together, and our company is much better than it would be if either of us had tried it alone.

WHAT'S AT RISK?

If you start your own business, you are risking several things. The most obvious thing at risk is all the money that you have and will put into the business. If the business fails, that is, if the business never makes a profit you will loose everything you have invested. If that thought bothers you, then don't go into business for yourself. Even if, in the long

run, you make money, if you are the sort that worries over every penny, it is probably not wise to be in business for yourself. Remember, as I said several times throughout the book, you will loose money for quite a while. This can make some people anxious and depressed. If your one of those people, this, or any other business is probably not for you.

Being in you own business means dealing with the uncertainty it generates from day to day. Even after you breakeven and begin to show a profit, you will never know for sure if the business will still be profitable next month. But if you are the sort of person that can live with uncertainty, perhaps even sees uncertainty as exciting and sort of an adventure, then being in business for yourself is the way to go.

Remember there will be no one to blame for the problems which will come up, but you. If you sit around waiting for someone to tell you what to do next, you will not make it. If you need someone to tell you what to do next, you really shouldn't be in business for yourself.

WHAT'S THE BENEFITS?

Many people go into business for themselves to make money. It's the wrong reason. There are many easier ways to make money than starting your own business. Many people go into business because they dislike following the orders of a boss, if you have difficulty following orders, you'll never be able to give them. There are as many reasons for trying self employment as there are people who wish to be sef employed. Many people find out that these goals are never reached. If you *know* you will be happy on your own, with the *freedom and responsibility* your own business will bring, then you know the benefits.

APPENDIX   1

MAIL ORDER COMPUTER COMPANIES

- *Austin Computer Systems*
  800-752-1577
- *Tri-Star Computer Corporation*
  800-678-2799
- *Iverson Computer Corporation*
  800-444-PC90
  - *Ergo Computing, Inc*
    800-633-1925
  - *Zeos International, Inc.*
    800-423-5891
- *Standard Computer Corporation*
  800-662-6111
  - *Northgate Computer Systems*
    800-526-2446
    - *Telemart*
      800-622-6659
  - *Swan Technologies*
    800-468-9044
    - *Gateway 2000*
      800-523-2000
      - *CompuAdd*
        800-288-3483
    - *PC Brand, Inc.*
      800-PC BRAND
  - *Micro Warehouse*
    800-367-7080
- *Computer Discount Warehouse*
  800-326-4CDW

APPENDIX 2

TYPE SAMPLES

DOT MATRIX PRINT:

```
-P088Z
Default character    ROM            1-1 OFF
Shape of zero        0 (Unslashed)  1-2 OFF
CG table             Italics        1-3 OFF
Protocol mode        ESC/P          1-4 OFF
Automatic tear-off   Invalid        1-5 ON
Country              U.S.A.         1-6 ON  1-7 ON  1-8 ON
Page Length          11 inch        2-1 OFF
CSF Mode             Invalid        2-2 OFF
Skip Perforation     None           2-3 OFF
Auto LF              Depend on I/F  2-4 OFF
Input Buffer         Invalid
 !"#$%&'()*+,-./0123456789:;<=>?@ABCDEFGHIJKLMNOPQRSTUVWXYZ[\]^_`abcdefgh
!"#$%&'()*+,-./0123456789:;<=>?@ABCDEFGHIJKLMNOPQRSTUVWXYZ[\]^_`abcdefghi
"#$%&'()*+,-./0123456789:;<=>?@ABCDEFGHIJKLMNOPQRSTUVWXYZ[\]^_`abcdefghij
#$%&'()*+,-./0123456789:;<=>?@ABCDEFGHIJKLMNOPQRSTUVWXYZ[\]^_`abcdefghijk
$%&'()*+,-./0123456789:;<=>?@ABCDEFGHIJKLMNOPQRSTUVWXYZ[\]^_`abcdefghijkl
%&'()*+,-./0123456789:;<=>?@ABCDEFGHIJKLMNOPQRSTUVWXYZ[\]^_`abcdefghijklm
&'()*+,-./0123456789:;<=>?@ABCDEFGHIJKLMNOPQRSTUVWXYZ[\]^_`abcdefghijklmn
'()*+,-./0123456789:;<=>?@ABCDEFGHIJKLMNOPQRSTUVWXYZ[\]^_`abcdefghijklmno
()*+,-./0123456789:;<=>?@ABCDEFGHIJKLMNOPQRSTUVWXYZ[\]^_`abcdefghijklmnop
)*+,-./0123456789:;<=>?@ABCDEFGHIJKLMNOPQRSTUVWXYZ[\]^_`abcdefghijklmnopq
*+,-./0123456789:;<=>?@ABCDEFGHIJKLMNOPQRSTUVWXYZ[\]^_`abcdefghijklmnopqr
+,-./0123456789:;<=>?@ABCDEFGHIJKLMNOPQRSTUVWXYZ[\]^_`abcdefghijklmnopqrs
,-./0123456789:;<=>?@ABCDEFGHIJKLMNOPQRSTUVWXYZ[\]^_`abcdefghijklmnopqrst
-./0123456789:;<=>?@ABCDEFGHIJKLMNOPQRSTUVWXYZ[\]^_`abcdefghijklmnopqrstu
./0123456789:;<=>?@ABCDEFGHIJKLMNOPQRSTUVWXYZ[\]^_`abcdefghijklmnopqrstuv
/0123456789:;<=>?@ABCDEFGHIJKLMNOPQRSTUVWXYZ[\]^_`abcdefghijklmnopqrstuvw
0123456789:;<=>?@ABCDEFGHIJKLMNOPQRSTUVWXYZ[\]^_`abcdefghijklmnopqrstuvwx
123456789:;<=>?@ABCDEFGHIJKLMNOPQRSTUVWXYZ[\]^_`abcdefghijklmnopqrstuvwxy
23456789:;<=>?@ABCDEFGHIJKLMNOPQRSTUVWXYZ[\]^_`abcdefghijklmnopqrstuvwxyz
3456789:;<=>?@ABCDEFGHIJKLMNOPQRSTUVWXYZ[\]^_`abcdefghijklmnopqrstuvwxyz{
456789:;<=>?@ABCDEFGHIJKLMNOPQRSTUVWXYZ[\]^_`abcdefghijklmnopqrstuvwxyz{|
56789:;<=>?@ABCDEFGHIJKLMNOPQRSTUVWXYZ[\]^_`abcdefghijklmnopqrstuvwxyz{|}
6789:;<=>?@ABCDEFGHIJKLMNOPQRSTUVWXYZ[\]^_`abcdefghijklmnopqrstuvwxyz{|}~
789:;<=>?@ABCDEFGHIJKLMNOPQRSTUVWXYZ[\]^_`abcdefghijklmnopqrstuvwxyz{|}~
89:;<=>?@ABCDEFGHIJKLMNOPQRSTUVWXYZ[\]^_`abcdefghijklmnopqrstuvwxyz{|}~ !
9:;<=>?@ABCDEFGHIJKLMNOPQRSTUVWXYZ[\]^_`abcdefghijklmnopqrstuvwxyz{|}~ !"
:;<=>?@ABCDEFGHIJKLMNOPQRSTUVWXYZ[\]^_`abcdefghijklmnopqrstuvwxyz{|}~ !"#
;<=>?@ABCDEFGHIJKLMNOPQRSTUVWXYZ[\]^_`abcdefghijklmnopqrstuvwxyz{|}~ !"#$
<=>?@ABCDEFGHIJKLMNOPQRSTUVWXYZ[\]^_`abcdefghijklmnopqrstuvwxyz{|}~ !"#$%
=>?@ABCDEFGHIJKLMNOPQRSTUVWXYZ[\]^_`abcdefghijklmnopqrstuvwxyz{|}~ !"#$%&
>?@ABCDEFGHIJKLMNOPQRSTUVWXYZ[\]^_`abcdefghijklmnopqrstuvwxyz{|}~ !"#$%&'
?@ABCDEFGHIJKLMNOPQRSTUVWXYZ[\]^_`abcdefghijklmnopqrstuvwxyz{|}~ !"#$%&'(
@ABCDEFGHIJKLMNOPQRSTUVWXYZ[\]^_`abcdefghijklmnopqrstuvwxyz{|}~ !"#$%&'()
ABCDEFGHIJKLMNOPQRSTUVWXYZ[\]^_`abcdefghijklmnopqrstuvwxyz{|}~ !"#$%&'()*
BCDEFGHIJKLMNOPQRSTUVWXYZ[\]^_`abcdefghijklmnopqrstuvwxyz{|}~ !"#$%&'()*+,
CDEFGHIJKLMNOPQRSTUVWXYZ[\]^_`abcdefghijklmnopqrstuvwxyz{|}~ !"#$%&'()*+,-
DEFGHIJKLMNOPQRSTUVWXYZ[\]^_`abcdefghijklmnopqrstuvwxyz{|}~ !"#$%&'()*+,-.
EFGHIJKLMNOPQRSTUVWXYZ[\]^_`abcdefghijklmnopqrstuvwxyz{|}~ !"#$%&'()*+,-./
FGHIJKLMNOPQRSTUVWXYZ[\]^_`abcdefghijklmnopqrstuvwxyz{|}~ !"#$%&'()*+,-./0
GHIJKLMNOPQRSTUVWXYZ[\]^_`abcdefghijklmnopqrstuvwxyz{|}~ !"#$%&'()*+,-./01
HIJKLMNOPQRSTUVWXYZ[\]^_`abcdefghijklmnopqrstuvwxyz{|}~ !"#$%&'()*+,-./012
IJKLMNOPQRSTUVWXYZ[\]^_`abcdefghijklmnopqrstuvwxyz{|}~ !"#$%&'()*+,-./0123
JKLMNOPQRSTUVWXYZ[\]^_`abcdefghijklmnopqrstuvwxyz{|}~ !"#$%&'()*+,-./01234
KLMNOPQRSTUVWXYZ[\]^_`abcdefghijklmnopqrstuvwxyz{|}~ !"#$%&'()*+,-./012345
LMNOPQRSTUVWXYZ[\]^_`abcdefghijklmnopqrstuvwxyz{|}~ !"#$%&'()*+,-./0123456
MNOPQRSTUVWXYZ[\]^_`abcdefghijklmnopqrstuvwxyz{|}~ !"#$%&'()*+,-./01234567
NOPQRSTUVWXYZ[\]^_`abcdefghijklmnopqrstuvwxyz{|}~ !"#$%&'()*+,-./012345678
```

INK JET PRINT

ID H

3.94 88/11/11

128K RAM

2836   Internal   Courier   10   12

!"#$%&'()*+,-./0123456789:;<=>?@ABCDEFGHIJKLMNOP
QRSTUVWXYZ[\]^_`abcdefghijklmnopqrstuvwxyz{|}~

2836   Internal   Courier   16.67 12

!"#$%&'()*+,-./0123456789:;<=>?@ABCDEFGHIJKLMNOPQRSTUVWXYZ[\]^_`abcdefghijklmnopqrstuvwxyz{|}

2836   Internal   Courier   20   12

!"#$%&'()*+,-./0123456789:;<=>?@ABCDEFGHIJKLMNOPQRSTUVWXYZ[\]^_`abcdefghijklmnopqrstuvwxyz{|}

2731   22706P   TmsRmn PS

!"#$%&'()*+,-./0123456789:;<=>?@ABCDEFGHIJKLMNOPQRSTUVWXYZ[\]^_`abcdefghijklmnopqrstuvwxyz{|}~

2731   22706P   TmsRmn PS

!"#$%&'()*+,-./0123456789:;<=>?@ABCDEFGHIJKLMNOPQRSTUVWXYZ[\]^_`abcdefghijklmnopqrstuvwxyz{|}~

2731   22706P   TmsRmn PS

!"#$%&'()*+,-./0123456789:;<=>?@ABCDEFGHIJKLMNOPQRSTUVWXYZ[\]^_`abcdefghijklmnopqrstuvwxyz{|}~

2731   22706P   TmsRmn PS

!"#$%&'()*+,-./0123456789:;<=>?@ABCDEFGHIJKLMNOPQRSTUVWXYZ[\]^_`abcdefghijklmnopqrstuvwxyz{|}~

2731   22706P   TmsRmn PS

!"#$%&'()*+,-./0123456789:;<=>?@ABCDEFGHIJKLMNOPQRSTUVWXYZ[\]^_`abcdefghijklmnopqrstuvwxyz{|}~

2731   22706P   TmsRmn PS

!"#$%&'()*+,-./0123456789:;<=>?@ABCDEFGHIJKLMNOPQRSTUVWXYZ[\]^_`abcdefghijklmnopqrstuvwxyz{|}~

2731   22706P   TmsRmn PS

!"#$%&'()*+,-./0123456789:;<=>?@ABCDEFGHIJKLMNOPQRSTUVWXYZ[\]^_`abcdefghijklmnopqrstuvwxyz{|}~

2836   Internal   Courier Italic   10   12

LASER PRINT

```
*********************
*                   *
*   Summary Sheet   *
*                   *
*********************
```

1. System configuration

Revision level	TANDY Laser V 2.0.0
Paper size Resident	LETTER
Total RAM	1536 KB
Available RAM	1201 KB

2. Default Values

Emulation	(1)	HP LaserJet Plus
Print Orientation	(2)	Portrait
Line Termination	(3)	CR=CR+LF, LF=LF+CR, FF=FF+CR
Auto Wrap	(4)	Disable
Font	(7)	COURIER 10

3. Fonts in system

COURIER 10	(*)	ABCDEFGHIJKLMNOPQRST
PRESTIGE ELITE 12	(*)	ABCDEFGHIJKLMNOPQRST
LETTER GOTHIC 16.7	(*)	ABCDEFGHIJKLMNOPQRST
CENTURY PS	(*)	ABCDEFGHIJKLMNOPQRST
COURIER 10	(*)	
PRESTIGE ELITE 12	(*)	
LETTER GOTHIC 16.7	(*)	
CENTURY PS	(*)	

4. History of errors

   No Errors.

POST SCRIPT © PRINT

Times
Times Bold
Times Italic
Times Bold Italic

Courier
Courier Bold
Courier Oblique
Courier Bold Oblique

Helvetica
Helvetica Bold
Helvetica Oblique
Helvetica Bold Oblique

ITC Avant Garde Book
ITC Avant Garde Demi
ITC Avant Garde Book Oblique
ITC Avant Garde Demi Oblique

New Century Schoolbook Roman
New Century Schoolbook Bold
New Century Schoolbook Italic
New Century Schoolbook Bold Italic

Palatino Roman
Palatino Bold
Palatino Italic
Palatino Bold Italic

Helvetica Condensed
Helvetica Condensed Bold
Helvetica Condensed Oblique
Helvetica Condensed Bold Oblique

ITC Bookman Light
ITC Bookman Demi
ITC Bookman Light Italic
ITC Bookman Demi Italic

Zapf Chancery Medium Italic

Symbol

αβχδεφγηιφκλμνοπθρστυϖωξψζ
ΑΒΧΔΕΦΓΗΙϑΚΛΜΝΟΠΘΡΣΤΥς
ΩΞΨΖ0123456789−=∴;϶,∕ ♣♦♥♠
(!≡#%⊥&∗)_+|{}[]:∀◇?−•+≠

Zapf Dingbats

These are the resident typefaces available in the QMS-PS 810 Turbo

For Additional Downloadable Typefaces, contact:

Laser Connection, Inc.
P.O. Box 850296
Mobile, Al. 36685
800-523-2696

APPENDIX   3

PRODUCT SAMPLES

STANDARD RESUME

ANNE M. ARENTZ
76 OAKCREST LANE
WESTAMPTON, NEW JERSEY 08046
(609) 877-3162

OBJECTIVE: Position involving sales management with a high
level of public contact.

SUMMARY OF QUALIFICATIONS

* Experience advising and solving problems.
* Good with figures and record keeping.
* Strong communication skills.
* Supportive team worker, committed and responsible.
* Work efficiently in a high energy work
environment.

RELEVANT SKILLS AND EXPERIENCE

Communications:

* Answered and directed incoming calls to:

Unemployment office

Macys' Department Store

Administrative offices

Arranged for travel, lodging for key level persons.

Administrative Support:

* Scheduled board meetings, staff meetings.

* Maintained personnel records.

* Maintained and upgraded FCC records.

* Typed edited correspondence.

* Hired and trained office staff and selling staff.

* Implemented new selling techniques increasing sales.

* Attended staff meetings.

TYPESET RESUME

WALTER F. LEISE
19 South Homestead Drive
Yardley, Pennsylvania 19067
(215) 493-7890

PROFESSIONAL EXPERIENCE

7/84 - Present   **ConvaTec, A Bristol-Myers Squibb Company. Princeton, New Jersey.** Presently Manager, Product and Device Design Group. Responsible for the direction and operation of engineering design group within ConvaTec. Other duties include budgeting, planning and coordination with marketing groups. Started as a Research Investigator with Squibb in 1984. In 1985 was appointed Manager, Wound Care Development (DuoDerm product line).

1/84 - 7/84   **Applied Digital Data Systems. Hauppague, New York.** Mechanical Design Engineer. Responsible for design, and mechanical layout of electronic components.

1/83 - 1/84   **Radiation Dynamics - A Monsanto Company. Ronkonkoma, New York.** As Chief Mechanical Design Engineer, established design and drafting departments for a new division, as well as, a process development department and prototype machine shop. Product and process designs were completed for radiation cured plastic products for telecom, medical, and electronic product lines. Established repair and preventive maintenance procedures for all existing and new production equipment.

6/74 - 12/82   **Burroughs Corporation. Yaphank, New York.** As Senior Engineering Designer, assisted electrical Engineers with the design of electronics packaging and casework. Prepared extensive mechanical layouts and investigated manufacturing alternatives. Selected mounting components for PC board applications, and provided assembly drawings and instructions. Acted as liaison to manufacturing for new products. Responsible for manufacturing troubleshooting and redesign when required.

PATENTS

US 4,344,612	Sheet Feeder Assembly	Burroughs Corporation
US 4,772,134	Container Port Assembly	Squibb Corporation
US 4,820,285	Bayonet Coupling for Ostomy Device	Squibb Corporation

These have also been filed in several foreign countries and have resulted to date in 8 equivalent patents. There are also 6 patent applications now pending, and 5 additional applications being filed for various products and processes in medical devices.

MILITARY SERVICE

7/66-5/70   **U.S. Navy - Naval Security Group.** Communications Technician. Honorable Discharge.

REFERENCES: Available on request.

NEWSLETTER

Volume 1   Number 1   **Spring 1990**

HEART & STRINGS

The National Newsletter of Depression After Delivery

NEW NEWSLETTER

We hope you like it! Thank you for your support!

❀❀❀

*The song from beginning to end
I found in the heart of a friend.*

...Henry Wadsworth Longfellow

ATTENTION TELEPHONE CONTACT AND SUPPORT GROUP VOLUNTEERS

When someone calls the national D.A.D. office for information, a "mom pack" is sent out right away. If you have been contacted by someone locally, you may want to have them call 215-295-3994 to receive the packet. These packs are available in English and in Spanish, thanks to the translation efforts of Alicia Medina, a volunteer in Florida. If you would like to receive a Spanish pack for Hispanic women in your area, please call the D.A.D. office and we'll be happy to send one to you.

Bi-Annual Eastern Regional Gathering

May 18, 19, 20, 1990 in Pittsburgh, Pennsylvania

Pittsburgh Airport Marriott
100 Aten Road
Coraopolis, Pennsylvania 15108

If you are a telephone contact, a part of a support group, interested in starting a support group or in reaching out in any way to families affected by PPD, come join us in a weekend of fellowship and sharing.

Saturday will be the meeting day from 8:00 to 4:00. Many attendees will be arriving Friday evening and staying until Sunday, so there will be lots of time for networking and fellowship.

For further information, to register, or if you would like to share a room, call the D.A.D. office at 215-295-3994.

For Hotel Reservations call the Pittsburgh Airport Marriott at 1-800-328-9297. Reservation deadline is May 4th.

How Our Childhood Affects Us

by Melanie Burrough, M.A.

Over 90% of us grew up in a family that was dysfunctional in some way. Amazingly enough, many of us survive unscathed. Some of us show signs of it as we tread through life...we have postpartum illness, we are or marry a substance abuser/alcoholic, we abuse ourselves or our children, we suffer co-dependency, we live our lives in secrecy from the shameful secrets of our past that we learned to keep, we laugh at everything even when we are really sad, we cry at everything even when we're really happy, we overeat to cope with our lives, we become anorectic to control our lives.

What is this buzzword of the 80's and now the 90's—Co-dependency? It is defined in as many ways as there are books on the topic, and there are plenty. One useful definition might be the one in Robert Subby's book *Co-Dependency, An Emerging Issue*: "An emotional, psychological, and behavioral condition that develops as a result of an individual's prolonged exposure to, and practice of, a set of oppressive rules - rules which prevent the open expression of feeling as well as the direct discussion of personal and interpersonal problems."

Another interesting definition was provided by Melody Beattie in her book, the "bible" of co-dependency, *Codependent No More*: "A codependent person is one who has let another person's behavior affect him or her, and who is ob-

...continued on page 2

107

MENU

Welcome to

TONY'S

FREEHOLD GRILL

**Fine Food
and
Family Service**

59 East Main Street, Freehold, N.J.

431-8607(8)

Index